# Federal Reorganization

CHATHAM HOUSE SERIES ON CHANGE IN AMERICAN POLITICS

edited by Aaron Wildavsky
*University of California, Berkeley*

# Federal Reorganization
## What Have We Learned?

Edited by
PETER SZANTON

CHATHAM HOUSE PUBLISHERS, INC.
Chatham, New Jersey

FEDERAL REORGANIZATION:
What Have We Learned?

CHATHAM HOUSE PUBLISHERS, INC.
Box One, Chatham, New Jersey 07928

Publisher: Edward Artinian
Design: Quentin Fiore
Composition and Printing: Theo. Gaus, Ltd.
Binding: Hamilton Printing Company


Library of Congress Cataloging in Publication Data


Main entry under title:

Federal reorganization : what have we learned?

   (Chatham House series on change in American politics)
   Includes bibliographical references.
   1. Administrative agencies—United States—Reorganization—
Addresses, essays, lectures.   2. United States—Executive
departments—Reorganization—Addresses, essays, lectures.
I. Szanton, Peter L.   II. Series.
JK421.F435        353'.073        80-29280
ISBN 0-934540-11-X


Manufactured in the United States of America

10   9   8   7   6   5   4   3   2   1

For David E. Lilienthal,
who reshaped government and made it work

# Contents

# Preface

The past quarter-century has been marked by a deepening anomaly: American society has assigned to its federal government steadily increasing responsibility and has regarded that government with steadily declining confidence. It was this tension that led Jimmy Carter to campaign in 1976 largely on a platform of government reorganization and reform, and to treat reorganization as a high priority once in office. But the constraints on governmental performance are tight. The Carter reforms have been modest, their effects marginal. Dissatisfaction with the performance of the federal government is likely to face each incoming President, and each cabinet member and federal agency head, for the foreseeable future.

It is striking, then, that if such an official, on entering office, looked to current learning for guidance in assessing the probable costs and benefits of alternative reforms of the structure or processes or staffing of government, he (or she) would find the literature remarkably thin.

Indeed, the standard wisdom appears to have less to say now than it did in 1940, when general principles of public administration seemed clear and well-settled. It then seemed axiomatic that the purpose of governmental organization was efficiency and that the means of achieving it were the proper arrangement of chains of commands, spans of control, specializations of work, and "neutrally competent" staffs. Those arrangements, in turn, were designed in the confidence that administration was distinct from policy making, that authority flowed down from the top of organizations while data and expertise flowed up from the bottom, and that legislatures established the law while executive agencies interpreted and applied it. The experience of practitioners and the analysis of scholars has cast doubt on the utility of each of those propositions; all now appear either simple-minded or wrong.

But few better propositions have succeeded them. Formulating and testing useful successors is likely to be the work of decades. It will require close-grained empirical study and should benefit from the theoretic perspectives of several loosely related fields: organizational behavior, policy analysis, industrial organization, public management. The essays presented here are no substitute for that work. They reflect no new empirical research, no novel paradigms of government, no radical insights into the nature of

ix

organization or management. What they offer instead is the attempt of a group of reflective practitioners to derive, from their own experience and from the larger record of recent attempts at government reform, a useful set of operational truths. Our main intended audience is the next wave of federal officials. But we hope that in trying to synthesize and clarify current understanding about organizational change in government, we may also stimulate students and scholars to challenge that understanding and to generate more discriminating, more powerful, and more useful truths.

The writing of these papers was sponsored by the Administrative Conference of the United States. Robert Anthony, chairman of the conference, and Stephen Babcock, its executive director, were helpful and congenial clients. James V. DeLong, research director of the conference, was a particularly supportive and encouraging critic. The editor and authors are indebted to Hugh Heclo and Richard Rose and, most of all, to one another for informed and helpful comment on earlier versions of these essays.

Peter Szanton
*Washington, D.C.*

# Federal Reorganization

# 1

# So You Want to Reorganize the Government?

## PETER SZANTON

Peter Szanton is a vice president of the consulting firm of Hamilton, Rabinovitz and Szanton, Inc. From 1977 to 1979 he served as associate director of the Office of Management and Budget, with responsibility for the Carter administration's reorganization studies. Szanton was previously a senior staff member of the Rand Corporation and first president of the New York City-Rand Institute. He served with President Johnson's White House Task Force on Government Organization (Heineman Commission), and as research director for the Commission on the Organization of the Government for the Conduct of Foreign Policy (Murphy Commission). He is the author of *Remaking Foreign Policy: The Organizational Connection* (with Graham Allison), *Not Well Advised,* and numerous articles on issues of public policy and organization.

Each succeeding chapter in this book addresses one major question about federal reorganization: When is it worth the effort? What are the alternatives to structural change? Are there general principles of organizational design? How should reorganization be managed? This chapter, more comprehensive and less original, cannibalizes the others. It attempts to construct a single framework for considering each question and all of them together. Since this chapter neither summarizes the arguments of the others nor fully adheres to their conclusions, it is an important advantage of this kind of cannibalism that while the cannibal is nourished, the victim is not consumed. Readers interested in particular subjects addressed in later chapters are urged to consult those chapters; they are the only expositions of the views of their distinguished authors.

## Why Reorganize, and Why Not?

The first rule of reorganization is to understand your purpose. Specifying a rationale is essential because some reasons may justify the effort; others do not.

Virtually all substantial reorganizations claim one or more of six objectives.* They seek to

1. *Shake up* an organization to demonstrate the decisiveness or managerial reach of a new executive or simply to place his (or her) mark upon it.
2. *Simplify or "streamline"* an organization (or the government as a whole.) This was the rationale for Jimmy Carter's promise, in the 1976 campaign, to reduce the number of federal agencies from 1900 to 200.
3. *Reduce costs* by minimizing overlap and duplication, achieving supposed economies of scale and efficiencies in management. This is the traditional rationale for reorganization and, at least until recently, the objective commanding greatest public and congressional support.
4. *Symbolize priorities* by giving them clear organizational embodiment. The belief that education was too important to bury in a huge department preoccupied with problems of health and welfare was the main rationale for the recent creation of the Department of Education.
5. *Improve program effectiveness* by bringing separate but logically related programs under more unified direction. This was the principal rationale for the creation of the departments of Defense and,

* It should be acknowledged that reasons never claimed also produce reorganizations or affect those undertaken on other grounds. The standings of key subordinates are probably the most powerful such reasons. President Johnson sought to make the Under Secretary of State for Economic Affairs simultaneously a Special Assistant to the President, and tried to graft part of the Federal Aviation Administration onto the Defense Department. The first intention is explicable only in the light of Johnson's personal relationship with Thomas Mann and the second reflected his desire to have Robert McNamara run the SST project. Similarly, President Nixon's awarding of the National Oceanic and Atmospheric Administration to the Department of Commerce rather than the logically appropriate Department of the Interior reflected his deep hostility to Interior Secretary Hickel.

more recently, Energy. It is also the reason for various systems of coordination among programs in separate departments or agencies.

6. *Improve policy integration* by placing competitive or conflicting interests within a single organization or subjecting them to processes of coordination. The brief and entirely unavailing attempt of President Johnson to merge the Departments of Labor and Commerce had this purpose.

These objectives partially overlap, and in most reorganizations, more than one objective is sought. The creation of the Energy Department, for example, might have been justified in part on each ground. But one or two objectives are usually dominant, and clarity as to which these are is essential to any judgment as to whether the effort is likely to prove worthwhile. The six objectives form a rough hierarchy. The earlier are trivial or quixotic; the later difficult but substantial. The break-even point comes directly in the middle. Depending on the degree of difficulty to be expected, objectives 4-6 may justify reorganization; objectives 1-3 almost invariably do not. Why not?

*Shaking Things Up.*

It is understandable and legitimate for an incoming executive to want to place his mark on his own office and perhaps on other units that directly support it. Then let him import a few trusted assistants and rearrange staff assignments as he likes. Neither is hard. Imposing substantial change on line operations—bureaus staffed with career officials and responsible for operating programs—will prove vastly more difficult. If the reasons for attempting it are powerful and the means well-chosen, the attempt may be justified. But simply establishing "who's boss" is a flagrantly insufficient rationale. And the outcome of so motivated a "reform" is likely to prove embarrassing. Bureaucracies do not regard line reorganization as a rub-down, stimulating and pleasant. To them it is surgery, involving anxiety before the event, trauma in the course of it, a lengthy convalescence afterward, and considerable uncertainty about outcome. The patient's capacity to resist the procedure, moreover, is impressive. Bureaucracies may stop a proposed reorganization by inducing interest-group or congressional outcries, or by discovering legal or administrative barriers. And what they cannot stop they can delay. All career bureaucrats have seen wave on wave

3

of senior executives come and go. The average tenure of cabinet officers is less than two years, and of assistant secretaries less than a year and a half.* And the initial priorities of senior officials are even less durable. So strategies of bureaucratic delay generally succeed.

## Simplifying Government.

The problem here is not that the goal is attainable only at excessive cost; this goal is an illusion. We are long past the point at which the federal government can be simple or readily understandable. Its jobs are too numerous, too large, too complex, and too inconsistent. It now undertakes not only the irreducible jobs of government—maintaining order, dispensing justice, conducting relations with other states, defending the nation from external threat—it now undertakes to ensure stable prices, full employment, environmental quality, equal opportunity, favorable trade balances, consumer protection, safety in the workplace, and so on. No government seeking ends as large, diffuse, and interconnected as those can be simple.

## Cutting Costs.

Here is a worthy and sometimes attainable objective that reorganization is too blunt and clumsy an instrument to achieve. The reasons are well described by Lester Salamon in chapter 4. Substantial savings may be possible when programs are eliminated, but the President's reorganization powers are usually limited to expressly preclude that result. At most, therefore, reorganization can reduce overhead or administrative costs, where potential savings are quite limited. Total personnel costs are just over 10 percent of the federal budget (and declining), and administrative costs are typically a small fraction of these. As Salamon points out, a recent study of $50 billion worth of federal programs concluded that 10 percent of total administrative expenses might be saved through reorganization—a sum amounting to 4/100ths of 1 percent of the total program costs.

So none of these first three objectives of reorganization are serious. The costs of attempting any of them will greatly outweigh likely gains. And

---

* Our government is truly remarkable in this and at a considerable disadvantage because of it. Secretaries of State tend to remain in place far longer than most cabinet officers, but Alexander Haig will be the eighth Secretary of State with whom Andrei Gromyko has dealt as Soviet Foreign Minister.

4

some costs may be unexpected. An important source of internal controversy in the first years of the Carter administration, for example, was the tension between the President's commitment to reorganization and his view of it as a means of streamlining the government. From the perspective of most of his senior aides, "streamlining" not only failed to advance any substantive policy goal but competed with policy objectives for the President's time and political capital. So the President's predilections to reorganize were steadily resisted by the officials closest to him, especially his domestic policy adviser and Vice-President Mondale. The result was that although great effort and substantial time were expended at high levels in the planning of ambitious change, the only substantial reorganizations proposed by the Carter administration were those made unavoidable by either explicit campaign commitments or powerful congressional pressure.* Even when the reorganizers sought to advance major administration policy goals—in the attempt, for example, to help make good on the President's promise of a new urban policy by consolidating urban development programs in a Department of Community and Economic Development—their political isolation denied them a timely hearing for the proposal.

Objectives 4-6—symbolizing new priorities, improving the effectiveness of related programs through unified direction, and better integrating policy by placing conflicting interests under the same oversight—are different matters; substantial and potentially attainable ends that may well justify reorganization.

* In the first category were the modest reduction in size of the Executive Office of the President, the creation of new cabinet departments of Energy and Education, and the redistribution of responsibility for enforcement of equal rights in employment. In the second were the creation of the Federal Emergency Management Agency and the International Development Cooperation Administration, the loosening of ACTION's control over the Peace Corps, and the revision of responsibilities for foreign trade. The only exception to the rule was civil service reform, where organizational change was an unavoidable result of policy change.

Meanwhile, much came to nothing. In particular, the extensive, presidentially commissioned explorations of possible cabinet departments—of Natural Resources, of Community and Economic Development, of Trade, Technology, and Industry, and of Food and Nutrition—were abandoned when no EOP champions could be found for them, and an ambitious set of organizational questions put by the President to the Department of Defense were studied slowly unto death by the department and then silently interred.

*Useful Symbolism.*

Creating a prominent new organization may meet an important political need. The creation of the Department of Health, Education, and Welfare (HEW) in 1953 powerfully symbolized the acceptance of federal responsibility for minimum standards of social welfare; it was accordingly treated by the press as a major event, though its substance amounted to little more than the application of new names and ranks to old programs. Similarly, the Department of Housing and Urban Development (HUD) expressed the 1960's recognition of a special federal responsibility for cities and the urban poor; and the Department of Energy embodies the priority now attached to reliable fuel supplies. As these examples suggest, symbolizing a national concern is far easier than relieving it. Still, institutionalizing a priority gives it visible expression, places it permanently on the national agenda, and creates an assured source of advocacy for efforts to deal with it.

*Program Effectiveness.*

Similarly, improving the effectiveness of government is a substantial purpose, and placing related programs under some form of common direction is a potentially powerful way of achieving it. It is well to emphasize the potential. Organizations create distinctive cultures. Organizations with long histories or important missions or records of great accomplishment generate independent cultures with distinctive values, practices, and traditions. They prove highly resistant to change. Thus, after more than three decades of subordination to a common superior, the three military departments still equip, train, and deploy themselves on only partially consistent assumptions as to the nation's most pressing military needs. Still, the existence of a Department of Defense, headed by a single Secretary, has clearly produced a better integrated and more effective set of military forces than would have been possible otherwise.

*The Integration of Policy.*

Finally, reorganization can help integrate policy. Arrangements that subordinate bureaus or agencies with conflicting interests to a common superior and thus force (or at least facilitate) comparisons and tradeoffs among them serve perhaps the highest purpose of government—that of mediating and resolving disputes among antagonistic interests.

It is a function more than ordinarily important now. This is a period in which two powerful trends have conjoined. The federal government has undertaken an enormous range of large, numerous, interconnected, and partly contradictory responsibilities. The maintenance of minimum levels of coherence and consistency in federal actions is therefore inherently difficult. At the same time, each of the central political institutions that historically have mediated between contending interests and imposed a measure of discipline on our pluralistic politics has weakened. Political parties, congressional leadership, and the Presidency have all diminished in influence as tolerance for authority generally has decreased and the power of special interests and the intensity of single-issue politics has grown. At bottom, of course, these trends produce a problem not of organizational design but of politics. However structured, staffed, or budgeted, institutions cannot wield a power that political forces deny them. But institutions may be well or poorly designed to exercise whatever potential they have. The central institutions of government, especially the cabinet departments and the Executive Office of the President, may therefore either partially offset or further magnify the effects of these trends.

It will prove especially important that their effects be offset if national politics in the next decade is dominated by issues like energy policy, whose resolution requires distributing not benefits but costs. No political system readily accepts costs. A system where authority is very widely diffused may reject them entirely. Faced with the problem of allocating costs, the tendency of a system of diffused authority is toward paralysis. Energy again illustrates the point.

So for those concerned about the effectiveness of the American government in the last decades of the twentieth century, an overriding task is to reconstruct those institutions that tend to resolve disputes rather than create them, that represent common interests rather than special ones, that look to the longer term rather than the pressures of the moment. The job is to strengthen those institutions individually and rebuild the linkages among them—linkages like those that previously tied the majority party, congressional leadership, and the Presidency.

## The Elements of Organization

Government organization is often thought of simply as a matter of *structure*

—the authorities, missions, and reporting relationships among various offices, bureaus, agencies, and departments. As Harold Seidman shows in chapter 3, the range of structures available in government is already vast, and capable still of useful innovation. But while structure is what is most obvious about organizational design, and easiest to chart, it is only one of three elements of any organization. A second is *resources*—the wherewithal an agency has (or does not have) to accomplish its purposes. Money is the most obvious form of resource and the most constantly fought over, but facilities and equipment is another, and personnel is a third resource and generally the most important. Finally, the *processes* through which an organization acts and by means of which it is linked to others also substantially effect performance. Processes may slow action or speed it, conceal disagreements or highlight them, suggest alternatives or suppress them, build consensus or dissipate it, facilitate oversight or deter it.

We distinguish these three elements of organization because each can be altered separately. Structural changes—establishing a new department or consolidating previously independent bureaus—are normally given greatest attention when reorganization is considered, but they are also the most painful and difficult to accomplish. Shifts in resources and changes in decision processes are generally easier to achieve and, depending on their form and purpose, may prove more effective. A sharp increase in the budget or in the number of authorized positions for a particular bureau can greatly strengthen both its programs and its policy influence relative to other elements within a department. Budget and personnel increases in an evaluative staff of the secretary of the department, on the other hand, can diminish the autonomy of particular bureaus. In neither case does structural change occur. In both cases the balance of influence is affected, and organizational behavior thereby changed.

Shifts in budget or personnel are normally easier to accomplish than major structural reforms, but changes in decision processes are generally easier still. And process changes—especially those that ensure better coordination—can also be far more useful. Indeed, effective forms of coordination are becoming the most broadly appropriate as well as the most feasible forms of organizational change.

The reason for this is that as governmental responsibilities have become more complex, they have also come to involve virtually all agencies. Energy

8

policy obviously affects not merely the Department of Energy but the Departments of State and Defense, Treasury and Commerce, Transportation and Interior, Justice, HUD and HEW—virtually all elements of the federal establishment. The number of departments not merely affected but with active responsibility for some substantial fraction of the energy problem is only slightly smaller—all of the above except HUD and HEW. When organizations share responsibility, they become, in effect, parts of a single system. The consequences for organization are profound. Reorganization has traditionally focused on structural change, whose dominating principle is that related programs should be placed cheek by jowl within the same institution. But the issues government now addresses (inflation, productivity, equal rights) cause widely separated programs to be related, and each with different sets of others, depending on the issue. Structural change is far too difficult and slow-moving to manage such shifting and multiple relations. Processes of coordination, far more flexible, are the only devices that can serve.

Yet attempts at coordination are regarded skeptically in government, and with reason: they often produce little but delay. Effective coordination requires authority. Its only purpose is to induce otherwise autonomous entities to act differently than they are inclined to do. In most matters, an agency's inclinations serve its interests; in important matters, they serve its important interests. The sheer logic of some larger purpose rarely suffices to alter such behavior. As Allen Schick suggests in chapter 5, therefore, "coordination" among equals is likely to prove only cosmetic. But if backed by authority, coordination can be an instrument of great power and relatively little cost. Successful forms of coordination, therefore, do not rely simply on the sharing of information or on attempts to sensitize decision makers to considerations of concern to others. Instead, they involve some form of supervision by a common superior. The superiority need not be overt or formal. An adroit staffer can coordinate the work of line officials of higher nominal rank. His authority may reside in nothing more than the shared perception that, if ignored, his views will be more decisively imposed by a still higher authority.

The operational question for a potential reorganizer, however, is not the utility of structural changes or resource shifts or revisions in decision process in the abstract; it is their comparative utility in some particular situation. It is to this question that we now turn.

## Choosing Among Alternatives

The choice of a particular form of organizational change should clearly turn on some estimate of its probable costs and benefits. Not much more can be said about costs than that the larger the number of people who believe themselves adversely affected, the higher costs will be, and the larger the number whose approval must be gained, the less likely they are to be borne. For these reasons, structural changes that require new statutes are, in general, the hardest to achieve. Restructuring through a reorganization plan is considerably easier. Passage of a statute requires powerful support in the Congress; approval of a reorganization plan requires only the absence of powerful opposition.* Easier still are changes that can be accomplished simply through Executive Order or presidential (or secretarial) memorandum.

Virtually all process changes can be put into effect through such internal directives. Though Congress may impose a process change by statute—requiring environmental impact statements to precede specified federal actions, for example—the inherent authority of senior executives is generally sufficient to impose substantial process changes on their own agencies without congressional action. Consequential resource shifts will generally require at least tacit congressional approval, through the budget process.

Considerably more can be said about the likely relative benefits of various forms of organizational change than about their costs. It may be most useful to discuss benefits in terms of the differing goals of reform.

### New Priorities

If the purpose of reorganization is to symbolize and advance new priorities, then the alternatives compare as follows.

* The exact limits of presidential authority to impose reorganization have varied with the terms of the long series of reorganization acts. In general, however, they have enabled the President, subject to the right of either house of Congress to disapprove within sixty legislative days, to restructure agencies and departments as long as he created no new cabinet department nor began nor ended any substantive program. From 1939 through 1979, 114 reorganization plans were submitted to the Congress; only 22 were disapproved.

*Structural change,* and in particular the creation of a new department or agency whose name and charter make clear its responsibility for the new priority, will normally have several effects. Most obviously, it will give the priority organizational embodiment. In establishing the Arms Control and Disarmament Agency in 1961, for example, President Kennedy gave institutional form to the policy goal of arms control and/or disarmament. Second, it creates advocates for the priority. Representatives of the new agency will assert its positions at the cabinet table and at every other forum for interagency discussion.

Third, if it brings under single direction related programs previously separated, the new agency may improve the effectiveness of those programs. Be clear, however, that this effect does not necessarily occur and almost certainly will not occur quickly. If important interests had previously wanted those programs kept apart, they will try to keep them autonomous within the new agency. Indeed, as a condition of getting sufficient political support for the new structure, the administration may have to give assurances, perhaps in the authorizing legislation, that such programs will be separately managed by their own bureaus or agencies and headed by officials devoted to preserving their independence.

Finally, the new agency may be able to make a more powerful claim for funding than its predecessor offices or bureaus could have done. (But historical evidence is mixed on this point and even theory is ambiguous. On the one hand, large agencies should be able to throw greater weight behind budgetary requests than the smaller and more scattered units from which they were created could have done. On the other hand, enhanced organizational position may be regarded, at least over the short term, as a substitute for additional budget, and a large agency with a weak constituency—the Agency for International Development, for example—may simply provide a large target for budget cutters.*)

* OMB has estimated that in the decade following the creation of HUD and the Department of Transportation, the programs of those departments experienced slower growth than they had in the years just prior to their creation. Similarly, federal funds for education appear to have been substantially reduced in the first budget year of the Department of Education. If maximizing budget is the aim, the prudent rule may be that it is safe to consolidate around a strong constituency but better to disperse programs serving a weak one.

*Process or resource reforms* can also symbolize and advance new priorities, though less dramatically. The design of a new program or redesign or expansion of an old one can focus far greater attention on the favored priority. (It may also provide employment for the groups most concerned to advance it.) Or a procedural device—an arms control impact statement, for example—can force decision makers normally insensitive to a particular concern to take at least formal account of it. Even greater weight can be given such a concern if officials representing it are assigned an influential place in interagency processes—given staff responsibility in working groups or assigned the chair in a decision-making forum, for example.

Yet process changes and resource shifts lack vividness, so when the purpose of change is to symbolize a new priority, the creation of a new agency seems more attractive. All the more so since, unlike a funding increase, it entails no budgetary cost and, unlike coercive coordination, it need not affront contrary interests. But a subtler cost is incurred. The natural dynamic of government is to spawn new entities. Interest groups seeking their own freestanding providers of funds or services, congressional committees or subcommittees bent on controlling a particular program, and career officials hopeful of influence and autonomy each seek separate organizations able to establish their own priorities, serve their own constituencies, and look to their own congressional supporters. Their combined influence is considerable; that is why the number of government organizations tends steadily to grow.

But this is a dynamic of fragmentation. Its end result is a disintegrated executive branch, in which little coordination or forcing of tradeoffs can occur outside the Executive Office of the President. So, despite its temptations, the tendency should be resisted; freestanding new agencies should be established only when the case for them is clearly persuasive. In the federal government only the Presidency has both the reason and the power to generate such resistance. Over the long term, probably no organizational responsibility of the Presidency is more important.

## Improving Program Effectiveness

When the purpose of reorganization is to improve program effectiveness, the relative merits of alternative forms of reorganization appear as follows:

*Structural change* can be used to create a new entity within which previously autonomous departments or agencies can be placed. The subordination of the military departments to the Department of Defense in 1947 is the most obvious example. Such a change can have two powerful effects: to improve the coordination of complementary programs, and to force comparison and choice among competing programs. What makes both these effects possible is, of course, the fact that programs previously independent now report to a common superior. To the extent that the superior can exercise genuine influence—to the extent, that is, that he controls appointments, promotions, and budget—he will have strong incentives to assess the major programs of his agencies and bureaus in terms of their relative contribution to the dominating goals of the department. In the case of Defense, to continue the example, one major purpose is the maintenance of effective and survivable strategic forces. That purpose virtually forces Secretaries of Defense and their staffs to consider Trident submarines, B-52 bombers, and Minuteman and MX missiles as technically differing means for achieving the same objective. Operationally they must supplement each other, budgetarily they compete. Secretaries of Defense, simply by virtue of their organizational position, feel obliged to insure that the duplication these systems involve is a largely useful redundancy, and that the plans for using them are complementary.

The power of inclusive new agencies to improve the effectiveness of programs that were previously autonomous is clear in principle; as suggested earlier, however, it proves hard to exercise in practice. Programs conceived, developed, and put into service by independent bureaucracies exhibit powerful tendencies to remain autonomous. The larger and more expensive the programs, the more powerful are the professional, economic, and legislative interests in maintaining their separation. Two consequences for reorganization flow from this. One is that proposals to assign previously independent programs to a common superior produce powerful opposition. The other, noted above, is that even when that opposition is overcome, the compromises necessary to create the new agency may have had the (intended) effect of insulating those programs from effective oversight or common management. Repeatedly since the creation of the Department of Defense in 1947, study groups, task forces, and blue ribbon commissions have suggested further integration of the armed services within the department. The organizational substructure that retains Secretaries of the Air Force, Army, and Navy, and substantial staffs reporting to them, and separate command and management structures in each service reporting to its uniformed chiefs as well, is of doubtful utility to the national defense. But it clearly helps preserve the separate identity of the services. All proposals for further integration have therefore met determined rear-guard actions. Significant powers have been taken from the services, but their management structures remain largely intact.

At least partial gains in program effectiveness may be achieved at far lower costs through *process change*. In 1961 President-elect Kennedy referred to Robert McNamara, his incoming Secretary of Defense, the conclusions of just such a task force as we have referred to. Appointed by Kennedy shortly after the 1960 election and chaired by former Air Force Secretary Stuart Symington, the group proposed that separate military departments be abolished. McNamara rejected this advice. He decided instead to rely upon a novel procedure, a Planning, Programming, and Budgeting system. PPB was a way of organizing the department's budget (and hence of framing the analytic work that supported the budget) in terms not of accounting categories but of major responsibilities or programs. The programs cut across service lines; they were strategic forces, air and sealift, continental air defense, and the like. This procedure placed Polaris (a navy program), and the B-52, and Minuteman (air force programs) in the same category: strategic forces. PPB thus provided a framework for evaluating those programs in terms of their relative contribution to a single mission. Since the Department of Defense prepared a single budget and the Secretary of Defense had a strong role in shaping it, PPB not only drew attention to the need to coordinate like programs and assess tradeoffs among competing ones, it also facilitated the efforts of an energetic secretary to force at least marginal changes in them.

Other procedures can be used to achieve the same purposes. A cabinet officer may ask his staff to compare similar programs whether or not they appear in the same budget categories. He can assign to bureaus that sponsor competing programs responsibility for explaining how they are related and why each is needed. He may sponsor competitive tests of alternative systems so that differences in performance can help force the process of choice.

For achieving greater program effectiveness, structural change and some procedural devices can be regarded, like the programs whose better integration they seek, as both competitive and supplementary. Fully amalgamating the armed services is probably neither possible nor desirable, but even if it were accomplished, some process like PPB would still have to be employed in the unified department. Structural change creates preconditions. It can weaken political and bureaucratic impediments to central direction. But it does not clarify how the power to direct should be used. For that purpose, analytic procedures are likely still to be necessary. Correspondingly, the procedures alone may suggest a decision without easing the political difficulties of enforcing it. It is often in combination, therefore, that these forms of organizational change have greatest impact.

The role of *resource shifts* in programmatic improvement is more limited. Budgetary shifts may be crucial in enforcing the results of tradeoff decisions between competing programs, but they can rarely help produce those decisions.

### Integrating Policy

Similar considerations apply, but in different degree, when the aim of reorganization is more coherent policy. Here structural change, and particularly the creation of broad-based departments, can have very substantial effects. If independent agencies whose perspectives and actions are inconsistent can be brought within a larger structure, their common superior can help mediate and manage conflict that previously would have either been left unresolved or managed by an agency of the Executive Office of the President, or possibly by the President himself. In attempting, in 1967, to create a Department of Economic Affairs in which the Departments of Labor and Commerce would be merged, President Johnson sought to achieve exactly this effect.

When they prove possible, such reforms help keep from the President's desk issues he does not wish to see there, and provide an arena in which they can be given far more sustained and careful attention. The staff of a Department of Economic Affairs, for example, would have more time, expertise, and incentive than any White House or Executive Office staff to manage, enforce, and monitor the effects of a decision on a change in the minimum wage, for example. The head of such a department, moreover, would tend to take a broader and less parochial view of economic issues than his Labor or Commerce predecessors normally could. Other things being equal, such an official would be more likely, therefore, to enjoy presidential trust, and to assume a significant role in the inner deliberations of an administration. Yet, the creation of such superdepartments, as we have noted before, is extraordinarily difficult. Johnson's proposal for a Department of Economic Affairs attracted little support but did generate fierce and immediate opposition from business and (especially) organized labor. It was abandoned without even a congressional hearing.

As a practical matter, therefore, better policy integration is more likely to be reached through improved decision processes than by structural change. As to second-order issues, the aim of such processes should be the accommodation of cross-departmental differences; in matters of great consequence the aim should be well-informed presidential decision. The processes may be formal or informal; they may involve extended debate at successively higher levels or move rapidly to discussions among cabinet officers. In either event they should seek a conscientious examination of alternatives and a rounded assessment of costs, benefits, and feasibility. Those attributes are hardly self-generating. It is therefore a presidential responsibility—arguably the President's most important managerial responsibility—to see to it that reasonable interagency forums and processes are established, that they are kept at work, that they provide him early warning both of issues he may want to resolve and of issues he may want managed by others or kept open, and that, at whatever level a decision is reached, it is taken only after its relation to the larger goals of the administration has been understood.

### How and When to Proceed

For an administration interested at least in exploring substantial reorganization, the threshold question is how to organize the reorganizers. There are several alternatives, each with long histories, as I. M. Destler describes in chapter 6. Though many choices must be made, the first and most decisive is between what might be termed "blue ribbon" and "no ribbon" status.

The first encompasses all publicly appointed commissions, task forces, and study groups containing independent members of some prominence, charged with determining what needs doing and why and how, and intended to report their conclusions publicly. The two Hoover Commissions are prominent examples. The no-ribbon approach involves a working group internal to the administration It may operate secretly, as did President Johnson's Heineman Commission, or seek both publicity and public participation, as President Carter's reorganization project did. But its distinguishing mark is that its members are chosen not for public prominence (though they may be prominent) but because they share the President's purposes.

As Destler suggests, the relative virtues of these two modes can be tested against some five criteria:

1. *Appearance of action.* Is establishment of the group itself regarded as a significant presidential response to a problem?

2. *Political weight.* Will the membership of the commission lend substantial political weight to its proposals?

3. *Amenability to administration influence.* How likely is the group to conform to the President's wishes?

4. *Capacity to learn.* Is the group likely to be guided by its own findings and deliberations, or is it likely to take positions previously formed?

5. *Capacity to assist implementation.* How actively will members help accomplish their recommendations?

Crudely, those criteria apply to the two modes as follows:

| Criteria | Blue Ribbon | No Ribbon |
|---|---|---|
| Appearance of action | Mid-High | Low-Mid |
| Political weight | Mid-High | Low-Mid |
| Amenability to influence | Low-Mid | High |
| Capacity to learn | Low | Mid |
| Capacity to assist implementation | Low | Mid |

In general, therefore, blue ribbon groups appear preferable when the appearance of action may be as useful as action itself, or when what must be done is fairly clear and the dominant problem is not analytic but political. Reciprocally, the no-ribbon form is superior when what needs doing is not obvious or when the sensitivity of the issue requires discretion and clear presidential control. But many decisions must be made in addition to the choice of ribbons.

## How Open a Process?

Another choice lies between open and closed processes of planning for reorganization. As mentioned, the Heineman Commission not only held its proceedings in confidence; its very existence was concealed for most of its life. It could therefore consult only senior administration officials and its own staff. The Carter administration task force assigned to explore the advisability of a Department of Natural Resources, on the other hand, circulated for comment to more than a hundred interest groups a detailed draft of its proposed memorandum to the President.

The criteria for selecting one of these extremes or, more likely, some intermediate position, are similar to those discussed above. An open process is better at demonstrating initiative, building consensus, exploring issues in detail, and addressing specific problems of implementation. It pays for those advantages, however, in time and staff energy expended, public criticism generated and—perhaps most dangerously—in the time it provides for opponents to organize. Conversely, a closed process is superior at generating unconstrained analyses of what should and can be done, better at maintaining the security of sensitive possibilities, and far faster.

The lessons of these opposing criteria are many, but the most important is simply that the more support of interest groups or the Congress is required, the stronger the argument for an open process. Where broad political acceptance is needed, much is likely to be gained and little lost by seeking that acceptance from the beginning. Where, on the contrary, a proposal is within the President's own power to effect, the advantages of a closed process may grow decisive.

## How Fast to Move.

A third choice involves timing. The truth that structural reorganization is painful, costly, and uncertain in outcome argues that it should not be undertaken until the evidence is clear that current structures are inadequate and that the changes proposed will actually improve matters. That clarity is rarely achieved early in an administration, before existing arrangements have been tested by new appointees and before the easy adjustments in process or structure have been tried. Delay also provides time for the careful design of change, for the participation of interested groups (including the career bureaucracy) in debating and modifying it, and for gauging the strength of political support and opposition.

But it is also true that the weeks just before and just after a new President's inauguration are the only period in which relationships are not yet established, procedures fixed, and egos committed to existing arrangements. "If you're going to do something substantial, for God's sake do it quickly." That was the message repeatedly conveyed to senior members of the Carter reorganization staff in their meetings with cabinet officers early in 1977. In *A Presidential Nation*, Joseph Califano has argued that Inauguration Day is in fact the only day on which the government can be substantially reorganized.

Moving immediately has many advantages apart from the fluidity of an administration's opening days. It gives a clear signal of managerial intent. If the changes have been decided upon before inauguration, cabinet and subcabinet officials can be chosen with the new design in mind and offered their jobs on the condition they support it. And early action can take advantage of the relative freedom of an incoming President, in the period just before inauguration, to focus on questions of structure, process, and appointments. Shortly afterward, the flood of substantive issues will preempt his attention and that of everyone close to him.

Under what circumstances should which arguments prevail? The more severe the inadequacy of current arrangements, the more certain a President is of the substitute arrangements he wants and the greater his capacity to impose a solution, the stronger is the case for speed and the weaker the arguments for caution. If the conditions for change are favorable,* in short, and the shape of desirable change is clear, then speed is advisable.

But some thought had better be given to the electoral politics of timing. Major structural reorganization takes several years to shake down. In their first year or two, new departments are likely to be less efficient, not more; to display lower morale, not higher; to afford greater opportunities, not smaller, for error, confusion, and scandal. So it is important that the shake-

---

* One of the circumstances that facilitates change is the presence of expanding budgets. In a period of growing resources, organizational change is relatively easy; substantial budgets can console organizational losers and generally lubricate the process. In periods of real budgetary stringency, however, the infighting over position and prestige will be all the more vicious.

down period have ended before the next national election campaign begins —or at least the next election in which the reorganizing President runs. A new President expecting to win a second term, and faced at the beginning of his first with a government he regards as seriously misshapen, might therefore decide to defer substantial reorganization for four years. Such a strategy would make it possible to use the first term to exercise the existing system, to attempt nonradical forms of adaptation, to design the kinds of changes required and begin building support for them. It can also employ the expectable turnover of personnel at the beginning of a second term to re-create some of the flexibility of the opening months of the first.

## How Broadly to Act.

The last of these "how" questions is how broadly to reorganize; whether the tail should be sliced off a piece at a time or the whole member severed at once. The applicable rule here is fairly clear. It arises from the truth that the opposition to organizational change is always more intense than the support for it. If opposition is broad as well as intense, reorganization will prove difficult. So, while genuinely interdependent changes must be undertaken together, unrelated reforms should be combined only if the conditions are especially favorable: the public demands wholesale change, or the President's power is at its likely zenith. Otherwise, one is simply providing opponents with allies.

## Principles of Organizational Design

In 1940 there was little doubt that the design of government agencies should be based on certain established, noncontroversial, and politically neutral principles. Prominent among these rules, drawn largely from the study of business organization, were that work assignments should be clearly specialized, related functions should be closely grouped, spans of control kept relatively narrow, and the neutral competence of career civil servants utilized wherever possible. The literature from which these rules were drawn assumed (or asserted) that governmental activities were largely autonomous, that information flowed upward from the bottom in organizations and authority downward from the top, and that policy making and administration could and should be separated.

Questioned by scholars, ignored by practitioners, and exploded by events, these principles and assumptions now lie in ruins. The question is whether any useful, general rules of government reorganization can be rescued from the wreckage. In chapter 7, Alan Dean attempts an ambitious reconstruction. Set out here are a more limited number of central principles that seem reliable and important. While they are not free of political coloration, their political intent—that of strengthening executive capacity to induce somewhat greater coherence and consistency in government—seems to the author wholly justifiable.

## A Principle of Inclusion.

The organizing principle of a department should be a national purpose or objective; and the broader, the better. The objective may have particular significance for an occupational group (as the advancement of agriculture does for farmers), or for a particular geographic region (as the assurance of energy supply has, in differing ways, for the Southwest and Northeast), but the organizing principle should not be service to a class or occupation or region; it should be a purpose of truly national significance and therefore important to more than one constituency. An organization that serves a single constituency will become its captive. An organization that serves several constituencies whose interests partially conflict will derive balance and leverage from the conflict. It thus becomes able to mediate private differences in the service of larger, public ends.

Founded on such a purpose, departments or agencies should be assigned as many as possible of those responsibilities that relate more directly to that purpose than to others. This test, of course, is hardly clear-cut. Many powers affect several purposes. Is responsibility for the education of American Indians more appropriately lodged in a Department of Education or in the Department of Interior, which historically has been responsible for Indian affairs generally? The answer will depend largely on political and symbolic considerations, but the substantive argument should hinge on whether the design and operation of programs of Indian education will benefit more from an administration sensitive to educational issues generally or from one more broadly cognizant of the problems of Indian life.

*Rules of Internal Design.*

With respect to internal design at least three general rules seem useful. The first is to avoid horse and rabbit stews. Consisting of one horse and one rabbit, such dishes taste a lot like horse. As Alan Dean argues in greater detail, no single element of any agency should so outweigh the others in personnel, budget, or policy significance as, in effect, to dominate the whole.

A second rule concerns spans of control. The classical injunctions of organizational design have asserted, on the one hand, that not more than roughly four to six immediate subordinates should report to any manager, but on the other that excessive "layering" must be avoided. Those rules point, of course, in opposite directions. It seems clear that, in government, holding layers to a bare minimum must take precedence. The reasons are several. Reducing the number of layers between a cabinet officer and his operating officials eases the recruitment and retention of able subordinates, speeds processes of decision and action, provides greater scope for initiative, and helps ensure that superiors perform different functions from those of their subordinates. These virtues are rare in government, where the frustrations of bureaucratic life and limits on government pay make the retention of able people difficult, where complex organizations slow action and deaden initiative, and where management often consists of superiors redoing their subordinates' jobs. But the heavy demands that flat structures place on senior executives will be unmanageable unless strong staff support is given them. Able staff can greatly amplify the capacities of an executive. Absent staff, a flat structure is equivalent to no structure; subordinates become autonomous, and an organization intended to strengthen programs or integrate policy does neither.

A final principle of internal design is that senior executives should have clear authority over all their subordinates. This is a gift, of course, that Presidents often have no power to confer. Constrained authority is generally the result of congressional insistence on direct relations between a bureau and a congressional committee, or of powerful support for the bureau (the FBI under J. Edgar Hoover, for example) from the public generally or from a special interest group. Presidents can seek to diminish or increase such constraints, however, and diminution should, in general, be their aim. When executives lack full authority over nominal subordinates, coherent management is attempted either not at all or only at inappropriately high and distracted levels. A responsibility that a cabinet member cannot handle will burden the Executive Office of the President, or the President himself, or—more likely—will simply be ignored. Sooner or later, a price will be paid. The FBI is again an example.

## Getting Change Accomplished

Organizational change is often attempted and rarely accomplished. One reason is that the nature of organization is poorly understood. It is imagined as a mechanism in which one component part can be readily substituted for another, or a design in which lines can be readily erased and redrawn. Both views embody two errors; they regard government as freestanding and separate, and they ignore the power of inertia. In fact, government organizations are, as Lester Salamon puts it, parts of frameworks of interest. They are tied to interest groups, political constituencies, regional concerns, congressional champions. They reflect the politics of the larger society and express an equilibrium of forces. And the personnel who make up those agencies represent histories, values, incentives, and skills of their own. These are difficult to change, impossible to change quickly. The consequence is that unless reorganizers understand the sources and strengths of current arrangements and advance their reforms with persistence and skill, their work will have little effect. New "superagencies," for example, will merely transform the independence of previously separate agencies into the autonomy of nominally subordinate bureaus. HEW was intended, in part, to create an integrated and consistent set of programs of social service, a task its secretaries not merely failed but barely attempted. They lacked both the managerial resources and the political strength.

### *Ease versus Effect.*

So it is important that the tactical choices we have discussed—open vs. closed, quick vs. slow, broad vs. narrow reorganization—should be assessed not mainly in terms of the ease with which reorganization may be achieved in form, but of their long-term influence on the implementation of change. Relying on statutory support from the Congress rather than executive discretion, for example, makes initial approval of a change much less likely. But, if achieved, it helps assure later congressional support. Similarly, participation in the design of reorganization by the permanent bureaucracies affected by it will constrain and delay any action. Once accomplished, however, it improves quite markedly the odds that action will in fact occur.

So reorganization had best be viewed as a branch of gardening rather than of architecture or engineering. As in gardening, the possibilities are limited by soil and climate, and accomplishment is slow. Like gardening, reorganization is not an act but a process, a continuing job. And like gardening, reorganization is work whose benefits may largely accrue to one's successors. A main reason why clearly useful reorganizations are not undertaken is that the costs of accomplishing substantial change—the political and bureaucratic opposition, the anxiety in affected agencies—accrue early while the benefits come late, after new arrangements have shaken down. So for those with short time horizons the incentives to sponsor change are weak. It is a rare reorganizer, therefore, who understands that the benefits of his effort will be conferred upon his successors and who undertakes the effort nonetheless. Rare, and correspondingly valuable.

# 2

# What Are We Talking About, and Why?

## PETER SZANTON

"Good men can run the worst kind of organization, and poor men can't run the best." So Dean Acheson put a prevailing attitude toward tinkering with the institutions of government: it just doesn't matter. This chapter, like those that follow, is founded on a different premise: the organization of government matters greatly (that's why reorganizing is so often proposed and so fiercely resisted), but its purposes and effects are poorly understood and (partly for that reason) it is extraordinarily difficult to improve.

The remainder of this book will attempt to enlarge our understanding of how organizations differ, of why and when reorganizations should be attempted, of how they might better be managed, and of whether there are useful general principles of organizational design. This chapter seeks to clear some ground for these discussions by raising and proposing brief answers to three questions: Of what do government organizations consist? Why do we establish them? How can one arrangement of government be regarded as objectively "better" than another?

### What Does an Organization Consist Of?

Dictionaries define organization simply as "an orderly arrangement." Correspondingly, government organization is often thought of as simply the arrangement itself—the structure of a department or agency or bureau. But anyone interested in affecting the performance of government must consider as well *what* is arranged or structured—mainly people, money, and equipment—and *how* the arrangement functions—its processes of decision and operation. Though the chapters in this book may stress one or another of these elements, we define government organization to include all three because (external pressures aside) the quality of government performance is determined by the interaction of all three.

*Structure.*

By structure we mean simply the existence of departments or agencies (and within them bureaus, offices, and individual positions) having particular missions, authorities, and formal relationships to other units, and the nonexistence of others.

*Resources.*

A unit's performance is affected not merely by its formal authorities and linkages but by the resources it deploys to support its mission. *Money* is obviously one such resource. Money may achieve a programmatic end directly (through transfer payments, for example) or indirectly (through subsidies of state programs meeting certain standards), or it may be used to obtain other resources (consultants). *Personnel* are another resource, and although highly capable people are not likely to be drawn to an agency lacking adequate formal authority or substantial funding, still the energy, skills, and values of its staff are normally the most important single determinant of an agency's performance. *Equipment* (tanks, computers, well-located quarters) is obviously a third form of resource. Some of it (tanks, computers) can be obtained in return for money; some (headquarters near the White House) cannot.

Agencies may also command powerful resources outside the government—a large or vocal constituency, broad public support for its functions—and these may greatly strengthen its hand within an administration and in the Congress. Such resources are largely ignored in this book since they are not subject to much manipulation by would-be reorganizers. Indeed, they may prevent would-be reorganizers from manipulating the other variables.

*Processes.*

The processes through which an organization acts are a third determinant of performance. There are processes for many functions: information gathering, planning, decision making, providing services, monitoring performance, coordinating related actions, evaluating performance, and the like. It may be useful to group such processes into three partially overlapping but distinguishable categories: (1) those by which *policy* issues are identified, analysed, debated, and decided; (2) those by which *operations* are authorized, managed, and performed; and (3) those of *internal maintenance* and management—by which staff are recruited, trained and advanced, for example.

We distinguish these separate elements of organization because they can be altered separately. The options in organizational change are not limited to revisions of structure—"shuffling the boxes" of organizational charts. The charts can be left untouched while significant change occurs. As Allen Schick suggests in chapter 5, attempting to change organizational behavior by affecting resources or processes may prove not only more effective than revising structure but far easier. That matters.

There are two polar attitudes toward reorganization. One is that reorganization resembles a good rubdown: it loosens the muscles, gets the blood flowing, and ought to occur with some frequency. The other is that structural change, at least, is major surgery, involving anxiety before the event, trauma during it, and a long period of convalescence thereafter, and that it should therefore be undertaken only when absolutely essential. We incline to the second view. Organizational change involves cost, pain, and temporary loss of function. And like major surgery two generations ago, its results are highly uncertain. The traditional estimate is that it was not until about 1900 that the random patient seeing an average physician stood a better than 50-50 chance of benefiting from the encounter. If so, reorganization is now at the level of development of medicine in, say, 1910. So the conservative rules of early medicine apply: above all, do no harm; avoid radical measures wherever possible. Altering the resources or revising the processes of an organization are often more consistent with those precepts than performing amputations or bone grafts on its structure.

There is a second reason for attempting organizational improvement largely through shifts in resources and changes in process. This nation and its government are gradually becoming a single economic and political system. The defining characteristic of systems is that changes in any part may affect the whole. To some degree, therefore, all major governmental programs affect all others. The dominating principle of structural change was simply to place cheek by jowl those programs having the strongest interrelations. This principle still has power, but much less than it did when those interrelations were few. Grouping some programs together now means, inevitably, separating them from others to which they are also related. As Rufus Miles has pointed out, "all government is a complex of matrices: if work is divided on one set of principles or axes, it must be coordinated on another." Increasingly, it must be coordinated on many others. We may therefore be moving toward a "poststructural" period when the key task in government organization will be one that only coordinating devices can perform: linking, for varying purposes, many sets of widely separated organizations.

## Why Organize?

Why are government agencies established?

### Creating Capacity.

The obvious answer is that one organizes to create capacities—to learn, analyze, decide, act, assess, relearn, and so forth. An organization arranges resources so that each of its major tasks can be assigned to persons or units trained, equipped, and instructed to perform them. It then adopts means to coordinate the work of these persons and units so that their separate efforts are orchestrated into a more or less effective and more or less coherent performance of the larger mission of the agency. The resulting capacity to accomplish multiple and complex tasks will greatly exceed the ability of any equivalent quantity of resources that are not similarly organized by skill, function, or rank.

### Capacity for What?

What capacities does government need? They appear to fall into at least two distinct categories.

Some government organizations manage fundamental and unavoidable responsibilties. Maintaining internal order, protecting the nation from external threat, and managing the nation's dealings with other countries are virtually the defining tasks of sovereignty. All nations therefore contain

28

Departments of Justice, Defense, and State, or their equivalents. Advancing the interests of agriculture or of education, on the other hand, while wholly legitimate, are not necessary attributes of sovereignty. They are choices, matters of policy. Departments such as Agriculture or Education, therefore, must be regarded as efforts to provide institutional voice and weight to a particular interest or perspective. At least, they symbolize the importance of such an interest to the nation. At most, they ensure that, through command of a budget and a seat at the cabinet table, the representatives of farming or schooling (or labor or housing) can actively advance those interests in the operations of programs and the making of policy.

A decision to create such a capacity—a decision, that is, to provide a particular interest with an institutional champion while not conferring comparable advantage on other interests—is a political decision. It has to do with who will get what (or, more accurately, with the probabilities as to who will get what). Even within the departments performing inherent tasks of sovereignty, many organizational decisions are, of course, political. Establishing an analytic staff in the office of the Secretary of Defense is intended to strengthen that Secretary's position vis-à-vis the uniformed services in debates as to budget and weapons. Establishing a Bureau of Human Rights in the Department of State is intended to ensure greater sensitivity to human rights considerations in a wide range of foreign policy making. As these examples suggest, however, the creation of offices representing one viewpoint in organizations whose characteristic perspectives are quite different requires that conflicts between them be somehow resolved. Organizations thus mediate and resolve differences within them as well as expressing differences between them. The question of the level at which such resolutions or tradeoffs are to be made is also, of course, a political one. That is why special interest groups seek to place representatives in the White House and, failing that, in the Executive Office of the President, and only as a third-best outcome accept representation at departmental level.

## What Is "Better" Organization?

But if decisions about organization are political decisions, how can they be judged good or bad? By what standards can some be objectively "better" than others?

## Supporting Policy.

The first answer is that subjectively better is good enough. The policy goals of an administration are legitimate simply by virtue of its election. The organizational arrangements that best serve those goals are just as legitimate. The only question is whether the cost—in political capital, managerial attention, bureaucratic disruption—of achieving those arrangements is outweighed by the benefits.

But beyond their fit with the policy goals of a particular administration, there are at least two characteristics that distinguish better from worse forms of organization. One is largely beyond dispute. The other is more arguable; it reflects certain political or constitutional values, but values we believe deserve support.

## Improved Efficiency.

Where one form of organization is simply technically more efficient—where, that is, it facilitates the production of a given service at lower cost, or greater output at constant cost, or where it speeds or simplifies the operations of an agency in its dealings with the public—then that form of organization can fairly be regarded as "better" than others. This is not to say that efficiency is an easy test. Except for the most straightforward of government services (issuing checks, delivering mail), efficiency may be very difficult to gauge. The service itself may be difficult to define fully, or the output hard to measure. Even where measurable, moreover, efficiency may be painfully difficult to achieve. Nonetheless, where one form of organization does in fact tend to increase it, that form can and should be regarded as superior.

## Greater Effectiveness.

Efficiency is measured within the boundaries of a particular program. It considers only the relation between inputs (the resources absorbed in delivering the mail) and outputs (the speed and reliability of mail delivery). Effectiveness must be measured outside the bounds of a program. It has to do with the comparative value of an investment in one function (delivering the mail) as against others (electronic transmission) that might serve the same objective. It has traditionally been asserted, therefore, that effectiveness in government is greatly facilitated by locating related functions within the same broad departments or agencies. Placing these functions together subjects them to the same oversight and control and so facilitates comparisons, tradeoffs, and coordination among them.

This view has its limits and its critics. The question of which functions are related or competitive with which others is not easy. As noted earlier, all functions, to some degree, are related to all others. It is also true that many functions have more than one purpose. The physical movement of large volumes of mail rather than the electronic transmission of the same information may have as a legitimate objective the employment of large numbers of people who may lack other marketable skills. So the tradeoffs between competitive programs cannot be analyzed simply in terms of any single objective.

Nonetheless, it remains true that the relations among some programs are far closer than their linkages with others, and that tradeoffs, though hard to assess, are not impossible. It remains true, therefore, that organizations that contain, at successively higher levels, successively broader aggregations of functionally related programs, and that are designed to enable executives to compare those programs in terms of their common goals and to act on the basis of those comparisons, can reasonably be regarded as superior to organizations lacking those characteristics.

It is now conventional to object that such effectiveness criteria are rooted, albeit unconsciously, in an executive bias. Though cast in terms of an apparently attractive and value-neutral goal, these criteria (so goes the criticism) strengthen one political actor—the President—against others: the Congress, the courts, state and local officials. The point is often accompanied by remarks about the pluralism of American society and the necessity for checks and balances.

The response of the authors of most of the chapters in this book, and certainly of this author, is that this criticism is useful only within sharp limits. It is helpful in clarifying the fact, for it is a fact, that the simple principles outlined above do tend to strengthen senior executives, and therefore the chief executive. It is not useful in suggesting that they are consequently wrong or inappropriate. While the value judgment reflected in those principles must be recognized, we would argue, it should also be gingerly embraced.

We make that argument on three grounds. The first is simply that power in the American system is now not merely shared as the founders intended; it is broadly diffused, indeed dispersed. Not only the courts, the Congress, and the states share power with the federal executive; so also do cities, ethnic and racial groups, industries, unions, and special interest associations of bewildering variety. And when many have the power to say no, no one has the power to say yes. Yet the national agenda, in the approaching years, is likely to be full of issues in which the dominating political problem is not who shall benefit, but whether to acknowledge that sacrifices are necessary, and how to allocate them, and how soon. Energy policy is a good example. In such cases, the widely distributed capacity to say no is the capacity to paralyze. Energy again makes the point.

There is another reason for believing that political power is now not only harder to assemble than the founders intended but more necessary to assemble as well. Our government was designed when it needed only to provide a limited number of "public goods"—defense, internal order, a currency, and the like. The task of government was not to lead or direct, but to maintain an equilibrium. The overriding concern was to prevent abuses of authority. But the tasks of the American government over the next decades are less likely to be those of equilibrium than of movement— especially toward a more productive national economy, a fairer* sharing of its fruits, and toward lessened vulnerability to external events. Those tasks will require a strong federal role, and therefore effective executive leadership. This is not an argument for leadership unconstrained—after all, the issue here is not amending the Constitution or abolishing the Congress or the courts, or diminishing their powers—but simply for broader and more integrated authorities *within* the executive branch.

There is a third reason for believing that a stronger executive, founded on relatively large-scale, functional departments whose chiefs have clear lines of authority within them, is an appropriate objective. An important and underrecognized function of government is to legitimate public decision making. Politics, by definition, is a business in which some gain and some lose. But losers accept their losses only when they regard the process of decision as fair. Broader departments, in which more of the considerations relevant to major issues can be raised and debated, tend by and large to facilitate better informed and more balanced decision making. They may thereby tend to contribute to public confidence that while government is founded on the pulling and hauling of special interests, it does not consist entirely of such contests, and that some institutions are designed to serve an illusive but transcendent value, namely, the national interest.

* The meaning of the term can be debated, but its political power and legitimacy cannot.

# 3

# A Typology of Government

## HAROLD SEIDMAN

Harold Seidman is a professor of political science at the University of Connecticut. During the Kennedy and Johnson administrations he served as assistant director for management and organization of the Bureau of the Budget. Seidman has advised the United Nations and numerous foreign governments on organizational and management matters and has lectured widely in the United States and abroad. He is the author of *Politics, Position, and Power: The Dynamics of Federal Organization*, and of several books and many articles on issues in public administration.

### The Absence of Principles

Government reorganizers and reorganization studies have tended to ignore the subject of institutional type, except for regulatory commissions and government corporations. While the President's Committee on Administrative Management, the Hoover Commissions, and more recent organization committees such as the Ash Council have developed principles to guide executive branch organization, one seeks in vain for comparable principles to assist in the choice among the rich variety of institutional types developed within our constitutional system: executive departments, Executive Office of the President agencies, independent agencies, institutes, commissions, foundations, authorities, wholly owned government corporations, "mixed ownership" government corporations, government-sponsored enterprises, government-organized "nonprofits," intergovernmental commissions, compact agencies, and a wide variety of advisory bodies.

The failure to develop principles stems in part from the fact that in analyzing institutional types we are often dealing with intangibles. What

33

people believe to be the virtues or vices of a particular form of organization is often more important than what they really are. There are no general laws defining the structure, powers, and immunities of the various institutional types. Each possesses only those powers enumerated in its enabling act, or in the case of organizations created by executive action, set forth by Executive Order or in a contract. Whatever special attributes may have been acquired by the various organizational types are entirely the product of precedent, as reflected in successive enactments by the Congress; judicial interpretations; and public, agency, and congressional attitudes. For some organizations, public attitudes tend to be based more on folklore than on fact.

In analyzing institutional types, it is necessary to evaluate the unique advantages and disadvantages of each type, if any, as they affect

Status

Public acceptance

Access to decision makers within the executive branch and the Congress

Competition for financial and personnel resources

Operating and financial flexibility

Distribution of power among the President, the Congress, the agency, and outside constituencies

Public accountability

## Constitutional Intent

The Constitution provides few guides for institutional choice. The intent appears to be clear, however, that all executive functions should be grouped under a limited number of single-headed executive departments. References to the "principal officer in each of the executive departments" and the "heads of departments" are significant.[1]

This intent is confirmed by the actions of the Congress for almost the first hundred years. In the first session of the Congress "organic" statutes were enacted establishing the Departments of Treasury, State, and War. All federal government functions except those of the Attorney General and Postmaster General were assigned to the three departments. Only four "detached agencies"—the Library of Congress, the Smithsonian Institution, the Botanic Garden, and the Government Printing Office—were created prior to the Civil War. Beginning in the 1860s three departments of less than cabinet rank headed by commissioners were established: Agriculture (1862), Education (1867), and Labor (1888).

The establishment of the Civil Service Commission (1883) and the Interstate Commerce Commission (1887) represent the first major departures from the original concept of organization within executive departments. In the case of the ICC a gesture was made toward maintaining the principle by requiring that the commission's annual reports be submitted to the Secretary of the Interior. The ICC was not accorded independent status until 1889.

The concept was ignored in establishing the Federal Reserve Board and Board of Mediation and Conciliation in 1913, and government corporations during World War I. Since World War I, the number of independent agencies, commissions, and corporations has multiplied rapidly. By 1937 the President's Committee on Administrative Management was able to identify over one hundred independent agencies reporting directly to the President. It should be noted that "independent" means outside of an executive department, not independence from the executive branch. Some progress has been made in reducing the number of independent agencies. The 1978-79 *Government Manual* lists fifty-five independent agencies, but this number does not include mixed-ownership government corporations, government-sponsored enterprises, nonprofit corporations organized by the government to provide contractual services, and intergovernmental bodies.

## Significant Differences Among Types

While one can search in vain for a body of principles or a precise description of the unique characteristics of each of the institutional types, an analysis of statutory provisions indicates that the Congress has followed a reasonably consistent pattern with respect to the organizational structure, powers, and immunities of each of the major types. Critical differences are to be found in those provisions relating to the composition of the directing authority (single- or multiheaded), qualifications for appointment, procedures for appointment and removal of principal officers, method of financing, budget and audit controls, personnel regulations, advisory councils and committees, and permanence.

The Executive Schedule Pay Rates provide the only official guide for ranking executive agencies. For example, the heads of executive departments are Level 1; the heads of major executive office agencies, the military departments, Veterans Administration, International Communications Agency, and the chairman of Federal Reserve are Level 2; independent agencies such as the General Services Administration and Small Business Administration and major regulatory commissions such as the Interstate Commerce Commission are Level 3; lower-ranking independent agencies, commissions and corporations (for example, the National Transportation Safety Board, St. Lawrence Seaway Development Corporation) are classified at Level 4; and bringing up the rear in Level 5 are minor agencies such as the Foreign Claims Settlement Commission. The ranking is significant not only in determining levels of pay but also in determining the rights to such perquisites as heavy sedans.

In selecting one type of organization, one is not necessarily precluded from using other types. Commissions, government corporations, foundations, institutes, and the like may be established as independent entities or may be organized as subunits within executive departments and agencies or placed under the supervision of department heads. For example, a majority of the wholly owned government corporations are organized within executive departments. Exceptions are the Tennessee Valley Authority, Export-Import Bank, Inter-American Foundation, and Overseas Private Investment Corporation.

## Executive Departments

No exact criteria have ever been prescribed by the Congress for establishing executive departments. In considering proposals for establishing new executive departments, the debate has generally focused on such issues as permanence and significance of program, degree of national commitment, appropriateness of federal role, scope and complexity of activities, numbers of personnel, and size of budget. According to the Bureau of the Budget, "departmental status is reserved for those agencies which administer a wide range of programs directed toward a common purpose of national importance; and are concerned with policies and programs requiring frequent and positive Presidential direction and representation at the highest levels of government."[2]

Executive departments remain the most prestigious of the organizational types, even though the principal assistants to the President and heads of executive office agencies may exercise considerably more power and influence than the heads of executive departments. Appointment as head of an executive department has always been assumed to carry with it membership in the cabinet. This is not true of other offices.

Establishment of an executive department is basically a political act. It is one way of expressing national concern in dealing with urgent problems such as the energy crisis or symbolizing national commitment and values. President Nixon's proposal to abolish the Department of Agriculture was interpreted as a move toward downgrading agriculture and reducing its influence in setting federal goals and priorities. Arguments based solely on administrative grounds—reduction in the number of independent agencies, improved coordination of interrelated programs, and more effective service delivery—may be advanced to support proposals for executive departments; they are rarely decisive in determining congressional action.

Except for the Tenure of Office Act of 1867, which provided that certain civil officers, appointed by the President with the advice of the Senate, should hold office during the term of the President and one month thereafter, the Congress has not placed restrictions on the President's power to appoint and remove the heads of executive departments. Each executive department has a single head. Statutes differ in specifying the President's authority to direct and supervise cabinet officers. Regardless of statutory provisions, it is generally accepted that cabinet officers are the "President's men." This does not mean that the President can exercise powers vested by law in cabinet officers or order them to exercise such powers. If a cabinet officer is unwilling to carry out a presidential order, then the President's only remedy may be to dismiss him.

Organization of functions within executive departments does not in and of itself enhance the President's power and ability to manage executive programs. Cabinet officers differ significantly in their responsiveness to presidential direction. Those with powerful clienteles such as Agriculture, Labor, Education, and HUD tend to be less responsive than those without strong constituency ties—Justice, Treasury, and State. The Department of Defense does have a strong constituency, but the Secretary of Defense tends to function as a presidential agent because of the President's constitutional role as Commander-in-Chief and continuing concern with national security.

Even constituency-oriented executive departments administer a wide range of programs involving a diversity of clientele interests. The Agriculture constituency, for example, is composed of a number of organized subgroups with divergent views on agricultural policy. Consequently, executive departments are less susceptible to capture by single-interest constituencies than smaller and more specialized organizations.

Constituency ties are important in influencing access to the President. There is recognized to be an "inner cabinet" and an "outer cabinet."[3] Executive departments assumed to be acting as claimants and spokesmen for their constituencies are seldom admitted into the inner circle. Complaints by cabinet officers who were denied access to the President were common during the Nixon administration and have not entirely disappeared.

Constituency-oriented departments inevitably are suspect because they share a mutuality of interest with the congressional committees representing the same constituencies. Heads of these departments must respond to direction both from the Congress and the White House.

Elevation of programs to departmental status may contribute to changes in public attitudes and increased attention to the program areas within the department's jurisdiction. There is an expectation that enhanced prestige and influence will be translated into significantly higher budgets. The extent to which departmental status affects resource allocation is unprovable.

A department does set the area of competition for budgetary and personnel resources for those programs included within a department. A program is likely to suffer if it is placed within a department where it will be at a competitive disadvantage. Proponents of a Department of Education believed that it was difficult for education to compete on equal terms with health and welfare.

Departmentalization provides an opportunity for establishing more effective executive leadership, cohesive policy direction, and coordination of interrelated programs, but it by no means guarantees it. Some executive departments are little more than holding companies housing a number of semiautonomous operating entities. The Secretary reigns but does not rule.

The first Hoover Commission recommended that "under the President, the heads of departments must hold full responsibility for the conduct of their departments. There must be a clear line of authority reaching down through every step of the organization and no subordinate should have authority independent from that of his superior."[4] The President and the Congress adopted this principle in the 1950s by proposing and approving a series of reorganization plans vesting in department heads the functions previously vested in subordinate officers and bureaus and giving them authority to organize and reorganize their departments. Exceptions were the Office of the Comptroller of the Currency in Treasury and the Office of Education and Public Health Service in HEW.

While lip service continues to be given to the principle of departmental organization espoused by the Hoover Commission, limits have been placed by Congress on secretarial reorganization authority in establishing the Department of Energy, and various nonorganizational devices have been employed to inject the Congress into the chain of command. The Secretary of Energy is prohibited from abolishing organizational units created by law or transferring their functions to other units in the department. Inspector Generals have been established in all departments and are required by law to report their findings to both the Congress and the department heads.

The legislative veto represents the most serious threat to secretarial authority. In 1973-77, 107 laws were enacted containing legislative veto provisions; and the number is growing. Actions of both the department heads and their subordinates may be subject to legislative veto. While ostensibly designed to control the bureaucracy, the legislative veto often enhances the power of the executive and congressional bureaucracies and undermines the authority of the department head.[5]

The permanence of an executive department may be challenged by requiring that it obtain annual congressional authorization for its programs. In 1972, for the first time in the history of the Republic, an entire executive department, the Department of State, was given a year-to-year existence.

### Executive Office of the President

The establishment of agencies within the Executive Office of the President is also sought by professions and interest groups as a means for maximizing access and influence and obtaining status and prestige. Scientists were unhappy with their eviction from the Executive Office when President Nixon abolished the Office of Science and Technology in 1973, and three years later were successful in having the office reestablished as the Office of

Science and Technology Policy. Outside pressures also led to the establishment of the Council on Marine Resources and Engineering Development.

The degree to which location within the Executive Office of the President enhances power and influence either within the executive branch or with the Congress is questionable. The power of Executive Office agencies is derived from the functions they perform—not organization location. Influential units within the Executive Office are those that provide direct support to the President in conducting *presidential* business or that control action-forcing processes such as the budget and legislative clearance. Establishment of the Office of Economic Opportunity within the Executive Office of the President did not enable it to function as an overall federal coordinator of the poverty program. Clearly OEO was not acting as the alter ego to the President.

A distinction needs to be drawn between the White House staff, which serves the personal and political interests of the incumbent President, and Executive Office agencies intended to serve the institutional interests of the Presidency. These functions are by no means identical, although the differences in recent years have been increasingly blurred. Presidents and White House staffs have sometimes been willing to trade off constitutional powers of the Presidency in order to gain an immediate political advantage. The Office of Management and Budget is not as well positioned as was the Bureau of the Budget to act as protector of the Presidency since it is often identified as the "White House/OMB," and its director has sometimes acted as if he were a special assistant to the President.[6]

At one time the Congress recognized that the relationship between a President and his Budget Director must be one of intimacy and trust. Consequently, the appointment of the director and assistant director did not require Senate confirmation. This special status was revoked in 1974, a casualty of Watergate. Except for White House staff, the heads of the principal Executive Office agencies are now all subject to Senate confirmation.

Senior White House staff have the easiest access to the President. At the same time they are the least accessible to members of the Congress. As a matter of custom, White House staff do not testify before congressional committees, except when personal charges are brought against them. For this reason, the Congress is likely to view as inappropriate the transfer of operating functions to the White House office or the transfer of OMB functions to the domestic staff.

The director of OMB and other institutional Executive Office units spend much of their time in meetings with members of Congress and are available for testimony. The Congress, however, recognizes their special role as presidential staff and treats them differently from department heads and bureau chiefs. It does not call on them as frequently for testimony and accepts the fact that they must look to the President rather than the Congress for policy direction and guidance.

Traditional concepts of executive branch organization have not been observed as rigorously by the Congress in establishing the constituent units of the Executive Office of the President as they have been in the case of the executive departments. Today the Executive Office includes a number of collegiate bodies such as the Council of Economic Advisers and the Council of Environmental Quality. The chairman of CEA reports to the President with respect to the Council's work.

The basic concepts were ignored altogether in creating a congressional agency, the Office of Federal Procurement Policy, as an autonomous entity within the Office of Management and Budget. Senator Lawton Chiles stated that OFPP "is a unique creature in that it reports directly to the Congress . . . and is not just an extension of OMB."[7]

The Congress has been unwilling to give the President a free hand with respect to the organization of the Executive Office of the President. It does recognize, however, that "as a practical matter, the President cannot be compelled to utilize a policy making and advisory apparatus in the Executive Office against his own preferences."[8]

## Independent Agencies

Independent agencies are not, as has sometimes been argued, "creatures of the Congress." The term is applied to all agencies established outside of executive departments. Independent agencies are, however, highly susceptible to "capture" by strong constituencies, particularly those with a single constituency that is economically dependent on government services and subsidies. Many are structured in such a way as to limit the President's directive authority and to provide de facto independence. The President may be required to receive and consider nominations from outside groups in making appointments, and exemptions may be provided from the executive budget and presidential regulations. Most vulnerable are agencies organized by clientele or geographic area rather than by major purpose.

Efforts to transfer the Small Business Administration and veterans programs to executive departments have been successfully resisted by clientele groups. Congress bowed to pressure from the maritime lobby by excluding the Maritime Administration from the Department of Transportation. It also bowed to interest-group pressure in separating the Farm Credit Administration from the Department of Agriculture and placing it under the direct control of the Agricultural Credit Organizations.

Generalizations about independent agencies are somewhat hazardous since they come in all shapes, sizes, and forms and have varying authorities and differ in their relationships to the President and the Congress. Some, such as the General Services Administration, are expressly subject to presidential direction and regulations; others, such as the U.S. Postal Service and Farm Credit Administration, are fiscally independent (expenditures are "off budget") and almost completely autonomous. Independent agencies may be accorded considerable operating flexibility and exempted in whole or in part from civil service laws and regulations, or they may be required to conform to all regulations generally applicable to government programs.

As far as independent agencies are concerned, the Congress does not believe that the injunctions against multiheaded agencies and limitations on the President's powers of appointment and removal apply. Several have been given all the trappings of a regulatory commission, including multi-member boards selected on a bipartisan basis with fixed, overlapping terms of office. Qualifications for appointment may be spelled out in detail, as for the Small Business Administration and members of the Farm Credit Board.

Independent agencies run the risk of being isolated within the executive branch structure, particularly those agencies that are highly autonomous and clientele dominated. Access to the President and executive branch decision makers is usually limited. As the administrator of a major independent agency, the Federal Aviation Administration, Najeeb Halaby found that he was handicapped in competing for resources and was likely to lose policy disputes with cabinet officers. Consequently, he became a proponent of a Department of Transportation.[9]

Despite their manifest limitations from the President's perspective, Presidents have found that independent agencies have certain advantages.

Establishment of an independent agency is a visible response in areas of significant public concern such as environmental protection and poverty. Where two or more executive departments are claimants for a program, it enables the President to avoid a difficult choice. President Franklin D. Roosevelt employed independent agencies to stimulate competition and prevent innovative programs from being stifled within old-line departments with deeply ingrained cultures and administrative habits. Independent agencies provided an opportunity to recruit staff outside the civil service and introduce fresh approaches.

## Foundations and Institutes

Foundations and institutes are employed principally for programs involving grants to local governments, universities, nonprofit organizations, and individuals for research in the natural and social sciences, or for artistic endeavors. The unique characteristic of these institutions is a governing board and an elaborate superstructure of advisory arrangements designed to give representatives of grantee groups maximum influence over the allocation of funds. Foundations and institutes may be created as independent agencies (National Science Foundation and National Foundation on Arts and Humanities) or within executive departments (National Institutes of Health).

Foundations and institutes are structured to exclude "outsiders" from the policy process. Scientists believe that only scientists are competent to make judgments about scientific research.[10] President Truman vetoed the original bill establishing the National Science Foundation because the proposed foundation "would be divorced from control by the people" and would deprive the President "of effective means for discharging his constitutional responsibility."[11] He took particular exception to the provisions insulating the foundation director from the President by two layers of part-time boards selected from persons nominated by organizations representing constituencies. Effective control of the NSF is vested in a twenty-four-member National Science Board appointed by the President after giving consideration to nominations by various scientific and education institutions.

Foundations and institutes are likely to resist the performance of functions that conflict with the basic values of their constituencies. NSF has been reluctant to expand its jurisdiction to applied research.[12] It was unwilling to act as coordinator of federal science programs even though directed by law "to evaluate scientific research programs undertaken by agencies of the Federal Government." Foundations tend to be exclusive clubs that limit membership to those within certain recognized professions.

Foundations operate on the periphery of the executive branch. Presidents do not look to them for advice on government-wide policies and their access to top decision makers is limited. Scientific and research communities do have access to congressional committees and may be effective lobbyists for foundation programs and budgets.

## Regulatory Commissions

Independent regulatory commissions were classified by the President's Committee on Administrative Management as the "headless fourth branch of government." While initially the Congress made no distinction between commissions and other executive agencies, commissions have been transformed into "arms of the Congress" by constituency pressures, custom, and Supreme Court decisions.

Marver Bernstein has identified "independence" as applied to regulatory commissions, as relating to one or more of the following: "location outside an executive department; some measure of independence from supervision by the President or a cabinet secretary; immunity from the President's discretionary power to remove Commission members from office."[13]

The number of commission members varies from three to seven. All, except the National Labor Relations Board, are bipartisan; and members serve for fixed, overlapping terms of office. At one time it was common for commissions to elect their own chairmen, but all commission chairmen are now designated by the President.

The ICC Act authorizes the President to remove any commissioner for "inefficiency, neglect of duty, or malfeasance in office." In the case of *Humphrey's Executor* v. *United States* (295 U.S. 602) the Court drew a distinction between an agency performing quasi-legislative and quasi-judicial functions and an agency primarily concerned with administrative or executive duties. It held that the President could remove a Commission member for the causes enumerated in the statute and for no other reasons.

Despite the limitations on his removal powers, until 1973 the President was able to exercise some influence over commission policies, administra-

44

tion, and operations through the OMB review of budgets, legislation, and data questionnaires and Department of Justice control of litigation. In 1973 the Congress amended the Alaska pipeline bill to (1) authorize the Federal Trade Commission to represent itself in civil court proceedings, and (2) transfer authority for review of data requests from OMB to the GAO.

In an effort to further insulate the commissions from executive control, the Congress in 1977 excluded regulatory commissions from the President's reorganization authority. In the same year the Senate Committee on Governmental Affairs recommended: (1) independent regulatory commissions should conduct and control their own substantive litigation, except for litigation taking place in the Supreme Court; (2) independent regulatory commissions should transmit any budget request to the Congress at the same time as they are submitted to OMB, as now provided for the Commodity Futures Trading Commission, Consumer Product Safety Commission, and Interstate Commerce Commission; (3) legislative reports to the Congress should not be subject to prior clearance by OMB; and (4) selection of top staff should not be subject to clearance outside the commission.[14]

To increase political accountability, the Senate committee proposed that powers be vested in heads of executive departments comparable to those now vested in the Secretary of Energy. The Secretary of Energy is authorized to intervene in proceedings before the Federal Energy Regulatory Commission that have a significant policy impact and to initiate proposed rule making.

Evidence has yet to be produced which demonstrates that an "independent" commission either assures more effective protection of the public interest or greater responsiveness to the congressional will. On the contrary, commissions have proved to be highly susceptible to influence by the groups that they regulate. Roger Noll argues that "independence serves primarily to insulate the agency from the general public."[15]

Dissatisfaction with the performance of regulatory commissions is evidenced by pressures both to "deregulate" and to subject commission actions to legislative veto. Legislation has been proposed that would provide for across-the-board legislative veto of commission rules.

Regulatory commissions are characterized in general by a case-by-case approach to regulation, emphasis on adversary proceedings, and complex judicialized processes and procedures. The process is deliberate and slow moving. Commissions do not perform well if called upon to promote the interests of economic groups or to plan, establish goals, and develop comprehensive policies to achieve goals.

Independent regulatory commissions are accorded a relatively low status in the Washington community. Their access to decision makers in the executive branch and the Congress is limited. Most complain about the unwillingness of the President and the Congress to provide the resources they believe essential to carry out their statutory responsibilities.

## Government Corporations

President Truman laid down the criteria for the use of government corporations in his 1948 budget message. He indicated that the corporate form of organization was generally preferred when programs were predominantly of a business nature, were revenue producing and potentially self-sustaining, involved a large number of business-type transactions with the public, and required greater flexibility than the customary appropriation budget ordinarily permitted.

The United States acquired the Panama Railroad Company when it purchased the assets of the French Canal Company in 1904, but it was not until World War I that the U.S. government became a business entrepreneur on a large scale and established the first wholly owned government corporations. The government today is engaged in a large number of business-type activities including the making and guaranteeing of loans; the operations of canals, railroads and airports; the purchase and sale of agricultural commodities; and the provision of postal services. All these activities have certain unique characteristics that set them apart from traditional tax-supported government programs: (1) the government is dealing with the public as a businessman rather than a sovereign; (2) users, rather than the general taxpayer, are expected to pay a major share of the costs for goods and services; (3) expenditures necessarily fluctuate with consumer demand; and (4) additional expenditures to meet increased demand do not necessarily in the long run increase the net outlay from the Treasury. Experience has demonstrated that enterprises with such characteristics cannot be managed effectively under an administrative and financial system designed to control entirely different kinds of government activities.

The distinguishing attributes of a government corporation are not inherent in the corporate form but stem solely from specific grants of power customarily included in corporate charters enacted by the Congress. Corporations are separate entities for legal purposes and customarily can sue and be sued and can enter into contracts and acquire property in their own name. Most corporations can "determine the character and necessity of their expenditures and the manner in which incurred, allowed and paid," and are thus exempt from most of the regulatory and prohibitory statutes applicable to the expenditure of public funds. Under the provisions of the Government Corporation Control Act, wholly owned corporations present business-type budgets, which are essentially plans of operations "with due allowance for flexibility" and are subject to a commercial type of audit by the General Accounting Office. The Comptroller General ordinarily does not have authority to disallow corporate transactions. A corporation is normally financed by one or a combination of appropriations to its capital fund, which are not subject to fiscal year limitations; borrowings from the public, Treasury, or Federal Financing Bank; and corporate revenues. Employees of wholly owned corporations are U.S. employees, but corporations may be exempt from civil service laws and regulations.

Most government corporations have boards of directors. The Tennessee Valley Authority, Export-Import Bank, and Federal Deposit Insurance Corporation have full-time boards. Others have part-time boards composed of both public officials and private individuals; some, such as the Pension Benefit Guaranty Corporation and Federal Financing Bank, have "in-house" boards made up exclusively of federal officials. In many respects government corporation boards are historical anachronisms since the government does not require a board to represent and protect the interests of diverse stockholders. The need for and usefulness of most boards of directors is highly debatable. The Congress abolished the board of directors of the Reconstruction Finance Corporation and replaced it with a single administrator because the board encouraged "buck passing" and "diffusion of responsibility." Existing corporations or quasi corporations with single heads are the St. Lawrence Seaway Development Corporation, Federal Housing Administration, and the Government National Mortgage Association. The Secretary of Housing and Urban Development, in effect, has been constituted as a corporation solely for the administration of certain public enterprise funds.

47

Use of the corporate form does not dictate organizational location or organizational relationships. Corporations may be established as independent entities reporting directly to the President, integrated within executive departments and agencies, or made subject to direction and supervision by the department head responsible for the functional area in which the corporation is operating. Specific actions that involve national policy may be subject to approval by either the President or the head of the relevant executive department. While accorded considerable operating and financial flexibility, wholly owned government corporations are not "autonomous" in the sense of having freedom from accountability to the President, the Congress, and the public.

Mixed-ownership government corporations present a distinct class of problems. This category should be reserved for programs that are in a transition to private ownership, but it has been employed as a device to escape budget review, as in the case of the Federal Deposit Insurance Corporation and U.S. Railway Association. Mixed-ownership corporations are not subject to the provisions of the Government Corporation Control Act requiring the annual submission of a business-type budget.

Mixed-ownership corporations have at times demanded all the privileges of a public agency without being willing to accept the responsibilities. Mixed-ownership corporations have been successful in maintaining at least a degree of independence from both the President and the Congress, particularly those that are self-financing and have a majority of directors nominated or elected by private stockholders, such as the Farm Credit banks.

Government corporations generally have a low profile and little political clout. The one possible exception is the Tennessee Valley Authority. Unless a corporation is financially self-sustaining, it is likely to experience difficulty in obtaining necessary resources.

The very fact that government corporations are "different" causes them to be viewed with suspicion. There is an inevitable bureaucratic pressure to eliminate diversity and insist on uniformity in budgetary, audit, and administrative regulations. Corporate flexibility has been seriously impaired by the imposition of personnel ceilings, annual expenditure limitations, and Comptroller General decisions classifying corporate funds as appropriated. These actions would appear to conflict with the letter and intent of the Government Corporation Control Act. The consequences are to be seen in the rapidly increasing number of government-sponsored enterprises and nonprofit corporations in a "twilight zone" outside the executive branch.

## Government-Sponsored Enterprises

To obtain financial flexibility and avoid onerous controls, the government-sponsored enterprise is now the instrument of choice rather than the wholly owned government corporation. Most recently, President Carter has proposed the creation of a tax-financed Energy Security Corporation as "an independent government sponsored enterprise . . . located outside the executive branch, independent of any government agency."[16] Government-sponsored enterprises include the Corporation for Public Broadcasting, Federal National Mortgage Association, Securities Investor Protection Corporation, and Legal Services Corporation.[17]

Government-sponsored enterprises constitute a very mixed bag. It is difficult to identify any distinctive characteristics common to such diverse organizations as the Securities Investor Protection Corporation and the Legal Services Corporation. Whatever other reasons may be cited, the overriding objective in establishing government-sponsored enterprises is to provide "off-budget" financing and avoid personnel ceilings and other controls applicable to government funds, contracts, officers, and employees.

The Congressional Budget Act has had the effect of significantly enhancing the value of off-budget status.[18] Off-budget agencies are not included in the aggregate or functional amounts set forth in congressional budget resolutions. The excluded outlays of government-sponsored enterprises have jumped from relatively small amounts in the 1960s to an average of $9.5 billion a year from 1973 to 1977.

Most government-sponsored enterprises are chartered either under the District of Columbia Nonprofit Corporation Law or the District of Columbia Business Corporation Law; consequently, they are subject to the provisions of both federal and District Laws. The Government Corporation Control Act required that all government corporations chartered by state or District laws either be liquidated or rechartered by act of Congress. There are a number of potential conflicts between District and federal laws.

Government-sponsored enterprises generally cannot be differentiated from government corporations or government agencies in terms of function, organization, and financing. Most government-sponsored enterprises have boards of directors appointed by either the President or a cabinet member, or consisting of public officials serving ex officio. Except for the Federal National Mortgage Association, National Railroad Passenger Corporation, and Student Loan Marketing Association, there is no provision for private equity investment in the enterprises. Financing is provided by appropriations, grants, government-guaranteed loans, and borrowing from the Treasury.

Employees of government-sponsored enterprises are defined by law as not being "employees of the Federal government." Such employees are not subject to personnel ceilings, conflict-of-interest statutes, and other laws applicable to federal employees. The Congress has imposed ceilings on the salaries paid to officers of the National Home Ownership Foundation, National Railroad Passenger Corporation, and the Corporation for Public Broadcasting. FNMA is directed to make appointments on the basis of merit, and the Legal Services Corporation is required to adhere to general schedule rates.

There is a diversity of provisions with respect to audit requirements. Some are subject to an annual commercial audit by the General Accounting Office; others are required to have an independent audit; and still others are subject to both requirements. The acts creating the National Parks Foundation and the Securities Investor Protection Corporation make no provision for an independent audit.

While government-sponsored enterprises provide an expedient means for cutting red tape, the blurring of the distinction between what is public and private creates ambiguities and raises serious issues of public accountability. There are many unanswered questions. What constitutional authority does the President have to remove a director of a government-sponsored enterprise? Do federal officials serve as directors of "private" corporations in their official capacity or as private citizens? To whom are federal officials accountable for their actions as directors? If a government-sponsored enterprise is not an agency and instrumentality of the United States, to what extent is it responsible to the President and the Congress?

Conflicts have occurred. President Nixon expressed fundamental disagreement with policies adopted by the Corporation for Public Broadcasting.[19] The Federal National Mortgage Association insisted that HUD Secretary Patricia Harris exceeded her authority in directing that 30 percent of FNMA's mortgage purchases be made in inner-city areas.

Government-sponsored enterprises are by no means insulated against partisan political pressures. Indeed, the very ambiguity of their position makes them vulnerable to such pressures. The Carnegie Commission on the Future of Public Broadcasting found that appointments to the board of the Corporation for Public Broadcasting were "highly politicized."

Given its ambiguous status, the government-sponsored enterprise cannot be held to account by the President and the Congress in the same way as other government agencies can. Attempts to maintain public accountability and control through the appointment of directors have not been effective. One scholar has noted: "Both the practicalities of life and the lessons of history lead to the conclusion that the appointment of Government directors to a private board cannot effectively protect the public interest against private abuse."[20]

### Nonprofit Corporations (Contract)

Nonprofit corporations organized at the initiative of executive agencies and financed under contracts with the government provide an alternative to government-sponsored enterprises. Relationships between the government and the nonprofit corporation are defined by the terms of the contract. Such organizations may be brought into being without specific legislative action by the Congress.

The emergence of the nonprofit corporation has been described as "one of the most striking features of America's postwar organization."[21] Initially employed mainly by the Defense Department and the Army, Navy, and Air Force to provide systems engineering, technical management, and analytical services, nonprofit corporations were organized solely for the purpose of entering into contracts with their government sponsors. In some instances, the government selected the "incorporators," who obtained a charter under the laws of the state in which it was to operate. Individuals invited to serve as trustees or directors were either picked by the contracting agency or selected with its approval. Except for grants made by private foundations to provide working capital, financing was provided entirely by the federal government.

Imposition of personnel "freezes" and inflexible personnel ceilings has spawned a new generation of nonprofit corporations to manage social demonstrations.[22] The advantages of nonprofits in designing, administering, and evaluating government programs are cited as

51

Ability to assemble high quality staff because of exemption from personnel ceilings and civil service regulations

Preventing the growth of the federal bureaucracy

Enabling different agencies to cooperate in an area of mutual interest without sacrificing jurisdictional responsibility

Providing insulation against outside pressures

Being less likely to perpetuate themselves

Combining the best features of the public, private, and nonprofit worlds

The speed, flexibility, and independence afforded by nonprofit corporations may well prove to be transitory attributes. When federal administrators become more concerned with contract administration than program results, the provisions of contracts are likely to be more and more restrictive. The Congress has taken a dim view of agencies created by executive action and has been critical of the freedom accorded some of the Defense-sponsored nonprofits, particularly with respect to executive salaries.[23]

Dependence on contract organizations may in the long run decrease the government's flexibility to deal with new and emerging problems. Its ability to redeploy scarce personnel resources is considerably reduced. Corporate employees cannot shift to another contract organization without sacrificing retirement and other special benefits. Programs cannot be altered or redirected without renegotiating the contract. Unless specifically provided in the contract, the government cannot fire or reassign corporate executives. Federal officers may well argue that they can be held accountable only for enforcing the contract, not for program results.

Presumably, nonprofit corporations broaden the base of political support by enlisting the cooperation of the private sector and appearing to be less bureaucratic than the government. Few of the nonprofits, however, have an independent constituency; and most are wholly dependent for survival on their government sponsors. Efforts of nonprofits to achieve a greater degree of autonomy by soliciting outside business have been criticized by the Comptroller General.[24]

## Intergovernmental Bodies

The Appalachian Regional Commission represents the culmination of efforts to devise an organization in which the federal and state governments could participate as "partners." Federal membership in the commission is limited to the "federal co-chairman" appointed by the President. Each participating state is also entitled to one member, who shall be the governor or his designee. Decisions by the commission require the affirmative vote of the federal co-chairman and of a majority of state members. No one employed by the commission "shall be deemed a Federal employee for any purpose." The regional commissions authorized under the Public Works and Economic Development Act are almost exact duplicates of the Appalachian Regional Commission.

While the ARC has enjoyed some modest success in coordinating activities for which it has received direct funding and in encouraging a regional approach, it has not been successful in planning and coordinating federal assistance programs within the region. Its record, however, is considerably better than that of the other regional commissions.

Intergovernmental agencies have limited access to the White House or Executive Office decision makers. Most governors have displayed little interest in the programs of intergovernmental commissions. Intergovernmental bodies tend to be orphans with neither the federal government nor the states willing to assume responsibility for their well-being.

### Conclusion

In evaluating the advantages and disadvantages of the various institutions, it is somewhat difficult to make definitive judgments. Significant factors such as a single administrator vs. a commission; organization by purpose, clientele, or geographic area; or source of funding may or may not be influenced by the choice of institutional type. Within each type there may be significant subtypes. For example, there are significant differences among executive departments and the powers vested in department heads. Nonetheless, it is evident that the choice of institution may well determine relationships with the President, the Congress, and clientele groups; the degree of operating and financial flexibility; the ability to compete for financial and personnel resources; status within the executive branch; public acceptance; and public accountability.

If there were a "pure" prototype of each of the institutions, it would be much simpler to identify significances and to select the type best suited to a proposed program. In choosing among the infinite variety of available institutions, one must be guided by probabilties rather than certainties. If evaluated in terms of status, public acceptance, access, competition for resources, flexibility, distribution of power, and public accountability, it is evident that one type of organization is more likely than others to produce the desired result. The analysis does not include contract organizations, which fall in a special category.

### Status.

Executive departments clearly have the highest status and provide the most visible expression of national commitment. Agencies of the Executive Office of the President rank close to executive departments. At the bottom of the scale are most regulatory commissions and government-sponsored enterprises with major independent agencies and government corporations in a middle position.

### Public Acceptance.

Judgments are difficult and depend on many subtle political variables. Often an agency that has the appearance of being nongovernmental—a government corporation, government-sponsored enterprise, or foundation—is more acceptable than a traditional government agency. This is often the case when the government departs from its traditional functions and undertakes novel programs, particularly those of a quasi-commercial character. If an agency is structured in such a way as to be susceptible to domination by a single interest group or profession, as are some independent agencies, it is likely to be less acceptable to the public at large.

### Access to Decision Makers.

In terms of access to the President and the Congress, clearly White House staff and the heads of Executive Office units and executive departments are in the most advantageous position. At the lowest end of the scale are government-sponsored enterprises, regulatory commissions, and intergovernmental bodies, with major independent agencies and government corporations in a middle position.

### Competition for Resources.

Executive departments with powerful constituencies are most favorably positioned in competing for financial and personnel resources. Least favorably positioned are regulatory commissions, intergovernmental bodies, and independent agencies without strong clientele. Special advantages are enjoyed by agencies such as the Farm Credit Administration or government corporations that do not have to depend on budgetary appropriations.

### Operating and Financial Flexibility.

Congress is more likely to grant operating and financial flexibility to government corporations and government-sponsored enterprises than to other institutional types. Flexibility normally includes exemptions from personnel ceilings and from most of the regulatory and prohibitory statutes applicable to the expenditure of public funds. It may include exemptions from civil service laws and regulations and laws applicable to contracting and purchasing of goods and services. If the intention is to provide financing outside the budget, the institution of choice is the mixed-ownership government corporation or the government-sponsored enterprise.

### Distribution of Power.

The heads of Executive Office units and executive departments may be regarded as presidential agents, although the heads of executive departments obviously differ in their responsiveness to presidential direction. Regulatory commissions popularly are classified as agencies of the Congress, as are some independent agencies and the U.S. Army Corps of Engineers. It was once said of the Atomic Energy Commission that it was administered by the Congress by and with the advice and consent of the executive branch.

Autonomous agencies with limited constituencies are most susceptible to "capture" by interest groups. As noted previously, the National Science Foundation was structured to exclude "outsiders" from the policy process.

### Public Accountability.

Government-sponsored enterprises, mixed ownerships, government corporations, and autonomous agencies such as the U.S. Postal Service have been exempted from many of the laws applicable to government agencies and personnel. Adequate measures have not been developed to assure that they are accountable to the President and the Congress and through them to the people. Comparable problems of public accountability are not presented by government corporations subject to the Government Corporation Control Act and by other institutional types.

## NOTES

1. Harold Seidman, *Politics, Position, and Power: The Dynamics of Federal Organization* (2nd ed.; Oxford University Press, 1975), pp. 221-23. Also see Ronald C. Moe, "Thoughts on Reorganizing Departments and Agencies," *Congressional Research Service,* 7 March 1978.

2. Statement of David E. Bell, director of the Bureau of the Budget, on S. 1633 to establish a Department of Urban Affairs and Housing, 21 June 1961.

3. Thomas E. Cronin, "Everybody Believes in Democracy Until He Gets to the White House: An Examination of White House-Departmental Relations," *Law and Contemporary Problems,* Summer 1970.

4. The Commission on Organization of the Executive Branch of Government, "General Management of the Executive Branch," February 1949, p. 34.

5. For a discussion of legislative veto, see Harold Bruff and Ernest Gellhorn, "Congressional Control of Administrative Regulation: A Study of Legislative Vetoes," *Harvard Law Review* 90 (1977).

6. The evolution of the Office of Management and Budget is analyzed in Larry Berman, *The Office of Management and Budget and the Presidency, 1921-1979* (Princeton: Princeton University Press, 1979).

7. Senate Committee on Governmental Affairs, hearings on the nomination of Lester Fettig, 5 May 1977.

8. House Report No. 93-106, p. 18.

9. Letter to President Lyndon B. Johnson, 30 June 1965.

10. W. Henry Lanbright, *Governing Science and Technology* (New York: Oxford University Press, 1976), pp. 145-146.

11. Memorandum of disapproval of S. 526, 6 August 1947.

12. Lanbright, *Governing Science and Technology,* p. 143.

13. Marver H. Bernstein, *Regulating Business by Independent Commission* (Princeton: Princeton University Press, 1955), p. 130.

14. Senate Document No. 95-91, 95th Cong., 2d sess., December 1977, p. XIII.

15. Roger G. Noll, *Reforming Regulation: An Evaluation of the Ash Council Proposals* (Washington, D.C.: Brookings Institution, 1971), p. 35.

16. Ronald C. Moe, "Government Corporation and the Erosion of Accountability," *Public Administration Review,* November/December 1979.

17. For a list of government-sponsored enterprises and discussion, see Harold Seidman, "Government-Sponsored Enterprise in the United States," in *The New Political Economy,* ed. Bruce L. R. Smith (London: Macmillan, 1975).

18. House Committee on Budget, "Congressional Control of Expenditures," January 1977, p. 77.

19. House Document No. 92-320.

20. Herman Schwartz, "A Dilemma for Government-Appointed Directors," *Harvard Law Review,* December 1965.
21. Bruce L. R. Smith, "The Future of the Not-for-Profit Corporations," *The Public Interest,* Summer 1967.
22. For a discussion of nonprofits, see Harold Orlans, ed., *Non-Profit Organizations:A Government Management Tool* (New York: Praeger, 1980).
23. House Report No. 574, 87th Cong. 1st sess., 23 June 1961.
24. Report to Congress on "Need for Improved Guidelines in Contracting for Research and Development with Government-Sponsored Non-Profit Contractors," 10 February 1969.

# 4

## The Question of Goals

### LESTER M. SALAMON

Lester M. Salamon is currently director of the Public Management and Government Studies Program at the Urban Institute and a consultant to the National Academy of Public Administration's Panel on Presidential Management. From 1977 to 1979 Salamon served as deputy associate director for organization studies in the federal Office of Management and Budget and was responsible for the development of proposals for organizational reform in community and economic development, transportation, agriculture, and economic affairs. Prior to joining OMB, Salamon was an associate professor and director of the Program in Urban and Regional Development Policy at Duke University. He is the author of *Managing Growth in an Age of Scarcity, The Money Committees, Welfare: The Elusive Consensus,* and numerous monographs and articles on problems in public administration and social policy.

*I sincerely hope that each of the reorganization plans not only promises but hopes to achieve greater efficiency and economy of operations. That is really the only reason for having reorganization authority.*
—Congressman John Moss, 1977[1]

"War," Karl von Clausewitz once wrote, "is nothing more than the continuation of politics by other means." The same, it can now safely be asserted, is also true of that peculiar form of warfare known as government reorganization.

This is no new discovery, of course, though it has long been downplayed, if not stoutly denied, in the more traditional theory of public administration and is still resisted in the rhetoric that regularly accompanies major proposals for organizational change. In these quarters, reorganization is more commonly portrayed as a branch of science than of politics, and its goals are associated more with economy and efficiency than with power and purpose.

This traditional view has in turn recently provided a useful straw man for a new school of administrative realism. In its zeal to set the record straight, however, this new school is in danger of throwing out the baby with the bath. Where the earlier orthodoxy viewed reorganization as chiefly concerned with economy, efficiency, and effectiveness, the realist school associates it with everything but. In the process, a false dichotomy has been created between the concept of reorganization as a means for improving government performance and the concept of reorganization as a means of gaining political advantage, a dichotomy that obscures the real goals and dynamics of reorganization and offers little guidance for public officials genuinely interested in improving the way government works.

The purpose of this chapter is to reassess the goals reorganization can reasonably be expected to advance in the light of our current understanding of the basic dynamics of American administrative behavior. The central thesis here is that reorganization can more usefully be viewed as a tool of policy than of administration. For reorganization to function effectively in this capacity, however, it must be integrated carefully into the policy process and approached with due regard for its political character.

To explore these points, the discussion falls into three parts. The first part seeks to establish the backdrop for analyzing the goals of reorganization by examining the basic political context of organizational decisions. The second part suggests a simple typology for thinking about the varied goals of reorganization and analyzes the dynamics of three basic kinds of reorganization identified by this typology. The aim of this section is to get us beyond the lengthy laundry lists common to most discussions of the goals of reorganization and thus lay the groundwork for more systematic understanding of what reorganization is all about. The final section suggests the implications these various goals have for the analysis and pursuit of reorganization in the future.

It should be noted that the term reorganization is used here primarily in a rather narrow sense, to refer to changes in the *organizational structure* of agencies or the *organizational location* of programs. This does not mean that such structural change is perceived as the only form of reorganization, or even the most effective. As will become clear, improvements in coordination and procedural changes in program operations can sometimes have as much influence on government operations as alterations in organizational structures. Yet the more narrow definition is utilized for the sake of focus and clarity.

One final note of caution is also in order. Although this chapter purports to analyze the goals and purposes of reorganization, in truth our knowledge about these matters is woefully inadequate. Serious empirical work on the real effects of reorganization is not only deficient; it is nonexistent. As a consequence, our knowledge base is at best fragmentary, impressionistic, anecdotal, and imprecise; at worst it is biased and inaccurate. Given the millions of dollars and thousands of person-years of effort that have gone into the generation of proposals for organizational change in the federal government over the past half century, this situation would be scandalous were it not so common. What it means in practice is that the discussion here must rely more on putative than documented effects, and on logic and intuition informed by observation and hearsay more than on solid empirical assessments.

## The Politics of Administration: The Context of Reorganization

That reorganization is a political and not simply a mechanical process is due in large measure to the peculiar character of the administrative process in American government. The starting point for any discussion of the goals of reorganization must therefore be an understanding of the central features of the American administrative state. Three of these features in particular seem especially important because of the implications they hold for the purposes of organizational reform.

### Power and Permeability

The first of these features is the highly fragmented character of the policy process in American government. Fragmentation of power is, in fact, the defining characteristic of the American political system. It was intentionally built into the structure of government through a system of "separated institutions sharing power" as well as the division of authority among levels of government, and has been further embellished by the committee system in Congress, by a generally weak political party structure, by a profusion of special interest groups, and by a variety of other factors.

This fragmentation of power does violence to the popular image of a unified executive personified in the President and responsible to a national electorate. In point of fact, there are multiple points of entry to influence the behavior of executive branch agencies. As Norton Long pointed out thirty years ago, power in the American bureaucracy does not simply flow down from the top along the chain of command; it also flows "in from the sides" and "up the organization to the center from the constituent parts."[2] While agencies can occasionally rely exclusively on the authority they derive from presidential direction, presidential attention is too dispersed and presidential political resources too limited to provide a satisfactory guarantee of agency prosperity over the long haul. Rather, each agency must perforce establish a modus vivendi with the key congressional and interest-group actors most concerned with its activities and ultimately in control of its fate. What this means in practice is that the policy process is fractionated into a series of largely independent "policy subsystems" linking portions of the bureaucracy, their related congressional committees, and organized clientele groups in a symbiotic state of equilibrium. In the process, a "structure of interests" comes to enclose each significant center of administrative discretion, challenging the formal hierarchy as a source of power and determinant of agency behavior.[3] Ultimately it is this "structure of interests," not just the agency itself, that must be the focus of attention when organizational changes are under review.

## Politicized Bureaucracy

The consequences of political fragmentation are in turn amplified by a second key feature of the American political system—the absence of a fully developed civil service concept. In theory, the civil service system should buffer agency personnel from the pressures arising from the "structure of interests" pressing in on them "from the sides." Such a situation would exist, however, only if careers could be made in the federal service generally, as opposed to in particular agencies, or if professional norms were strong enough to counter more narrow agency and group pressures. If this were the case, personnel would be rewarded for their neutral competence, their ability to carry out the public's business efficiently and effectively or their adherence to professional standards, regardless of the implications for the future of any particular agency or its clientele groups.

Although lip service is regularly paid to this ideal, reality diverges from it sharply. In point of fact, civil service mobility among agencies is limited at best and declines rather than increases the more senior the professional.[4] What is more, professional norms themselves often acquire an agency coloration. Most civil servants consequently know that their careers are intimately tied to the fate of their agencies. Since the fate of their agencies is in turn tied to a network of outside interests and congressional allies, the prudent civil servant must consequently be concerned not only about the execution of the laws but also about the mobilization of political support. Indeed, the survival, growth, and independence of the agency can frequently be of more importance to career civil servants than to their erstwhile allies in the Congress, in interest groups, or elsewhere. Far from passively responding to outside political pressures, career bureaucrats must be concerned to anticipate client needs and shape and help generate outside demands.

### Agency Ethos and Personality

These first two features of American administrative behavior lead directly to a third: the development at the bureau or agency level of a distinctive culture or ethos, a more or less explicit set of norms and beliefs that defines the agency's mission and its modus operandi.[5] Such norms and beliefs are present in all organizations. They function to give agency cadre a sense of identity and common purpose and thus help encourage uniformity and coherence in task accomplishment.

Because of the fragmentation of power and the absence of a fully developed civil service concept, the particular content of agency ethos in the federal establishment is importantly shaped by the content of the agency's task and by the "structure of interests" with which the agency consequently regularly interacts. As Harold Seidman has put it, "government agencies are social institutions" with their own personalities and outlooks.[6] And these personalities are shaped, chameleonlike by the environment in which the agency operates. Agency ethos is thus the invisible force that keeps agency behavior in line with external expectations.

If it is invisible, however, agency ethos is hardly inadvertent or accidental. It is typically firmly institutionalized in formal agency recruitment, socialization, and leadership succession processes. Public organizations do not merely draw their career personnel from a general civil service pool, or promote by applying merit standards to a limitless universe of qualified applicants. Rather, the dominant cadre faction begins with certain expectations about the kind of person they believe will "fit in" in the organization and thus maintain it over time. They then develop the procedures to find them in spite of, rather than by means of, civil service regulations. They also develop definite processes for socialization and prescribe career patterns that shape and mold candidates for top positions.

Because public programs almost always leave a substantial amount of administrative discretion, organizational ethos can importantly affect the ultimate content of public activities. While a rose is always a rose, the same is not true of a public program. A single statute can create quite different programs depending on where authority for its implementation is vested. In this way are the dynamics of administrative politics translated into the content of governmental action.

### The Goals of Reorganization: A Framework for Analysis

Given these dynamics of the administrative process in American government, it should be clear why reorganization is so complex—and so important—a process. Because they affect so rich a network of relationships, reorganizations serve a host of different purposes, often at the same time. Making sense of the goals of reorganization is therefore no mean undertaking. Indeed, reorganizations seem to come in as many different varieties as Heinz' pickles. Harvey Mansfield, for example, has identified nine different potential objectives of reorganization, ranging from upgrading or downgrading the status of particular programs to accommodating technological innovations.[7] Harold Seidman has identified eleven additional objectives, and Rufus Miles eight more.[8]

Under these circumstances, analytical clarity requires some effort to group and sort the various purposes of reorganization into a manageable set of categories. While any such categorization does some violence to the rich diversity of actual experience, it is essential if any real progress is to be made in thinking analytically about the reorganization process.

Regrettably, such categorization has not figured prominently in the existing literature on reorganization, which has tended either to throw all reorganizations into the same analytical pot or to treat each as *sui generis* and develop lengthy laundry lists of possible purposes. Nevertheless, this literature, coupled with the discussion above, does make it possible to distinguish three major "types" of reorganization goals. According to this typology, reorganizations can be undertaken in pursuit of (1) economy and efficiency, (2) policy effectiveness, or (3) tactical political advantage. Each of these goals is associated, moreover, with a particular focus of attention, a particular set of hypotheses about the effects of various types of organizational change, and a particular set of political dynamics. Although any particular reorganization proposal may include elements of all three types, and although each type masks a number of more detailed purposes, this typology provides a useful analytical framework that can help unravel some of the confusion that persists about reorganization and sort out some of the underlying issues involved. To see this, let us examine each of these broad types of reorganization in turn.

## Reorganizing for Economy and Efficiency

The most often expected, though least often delivered, objective of reorganization is economy and efficiency. Economy and efficiency are, in fact, the official rationales for reorganization. The act of Congress creating the first "Hoover Commission" in 1947, for example, cited as justification "the policy of Congress to promote economy, efficiency, and improved service in the transaction of the public business." Similar language has been incorporated as the primary goal of reorganization in every reorganization statute before and since. More than that, successive versions of the basic reorganization authority have put Presidents under increasing pressure to offer tangible evidence of the savings and efficiencies anticipated from reorganization proposals, and Congress has made a point of insisting on such evidence. When OMB officials failed to supply detailed estimates in connection with a modest 1977 proposal, for example, several members reacted with harsh indignation. "I would like to reemphasize the concern of the members of this committee that we do not want just new boilerplate language in Presidential messages but we really do want an itemization," trumpeted Congressman John Erlenborn.[9] "Maybe you can have savings which will result later," noted Congressman Frank Horton, "but you are going to have to make some sort of estimate or give us something much more concrete than just saying down the road someplace we are going to have a good administrator and he is going to do a good job, and he will do this and that."[10]

Though alternately a source of bemusement and despair among the professional denizens of government reform, this intense congressional appetite for savings from reorganization reflects some rather important political considerations. Economy and efficiency are, after all, potent political symbols. What is more, they are concrete, tangible, and easy to explain. They thus provide the kind of incontestable ammunition that supporters of reorganizations need to counter the opposition of those wedded to the status quo.

Most important, perhaps, the economy-efficiency argument rests on some straightforward, common-sense notions. The central focus for this form of reorganization is on the input side of government activity. The basic notion is that government is failing to capture important economies of scale because of *duplication of effort*. Such duplication is commonly associated not only with basic housekeeping functions (e.g., supply, personnel management, administrative support) but also with more program-specific activities (e.g., the duplication of appraisal functions among the housing programs administered by the Department of Housing and Urban Development, Veterans Administration, and Farmers' Home Administration). Closely related to this basic notion, moreover, is a corollary that focuses on the unnecessary burdens that duplication of effort imposes on the *users* of government services in the form of conflicting or overlapping requirements, information costs, grantsmanship efforts, and the like. The classic example here is the "wasteful conflict and duplication" among federal land agencies cited by the first Hoover Commission. According to the commission, ranchers who run their livestock on both national forest pastures and land in public grazing districts must, because of this duplication, "obtain separate permits with different terms and conditions from the different Federal agencies, and their grazing resources and livestock plans must be reviewed by each agency."[11]

The standard reorganization cure for these problems found classic expression in the first Hoover Commission's dictum to place "related functions cheek-by-jowl." In the Hoover Commission's view, "this is the *first necessity* for the establishment of efficient and economical functioning of the government."[12] Its contribution to efficiency can take a variety of forms:

(1) a reduction in outright duplication of activities; (2) a corresponding reduction in overhead costs through pooling of administrative services, especially in the field; and (3) a reduction in the administrative costs borne by program users.

Of all the forms of reorganization, however, reorganization for efficiency and economy is clearly the most discredited. "We have got to get over the notion that the purpose of reorganization is economy," President Franklin Roosevelt told Luther Gulick and Louis Brownlow more than forty years ago; and most students of the subject would readily agree today.[13] The reasons for this are numerous. In the first place, the aggregate sums available to be saved in the administration of government services are far smaller than commonly acknowledged. Arthur Holcombe recognized this point as early as 1921, when he reported that "a glance at the published statements of appropriations suggests that the possible savings to be obtained by a more economical arrangement of the administrative agencies outside the military and naval establishments cannot exceed a fraction of one percent of the total annual expenditures."[14] Despite the massive growth in government during the intervening sixty years, the same point applies today. As of 1978, for example, the total civilian personnel costs of the federal government came to $50 billion out of a total federal budget of $451 billion, or 11 percent of the total.[15] Far from increasing, moreover, this percentage has been decreasing over the years as the nature of federal programs has changed. In fact, federal employment over the past thirty years has grown only half as fast as the real growth of federal expenditures. Even considering the improvement in federal pay scales, therefore, federal personnel costs as a proportion of total federal outlays have declined substantially. Between 1955 and 1978, for example, this figure dropped from 15 percent to 11 percent, a decline of almost 30 percent.[16] Under the circumstances, the opportunities for administrative savings through reorganization may be quite limited. For example, a recent reorganization study of the $50 billion federal community and economic development programs concluded that 10 percent of total administrative expenses could potentially be saved through reorganization. But this still came to less than $20 million in savings, or 4/100th of 1 percent of the total program costs.[17]

Not only are the aggregate administrative savings potentially available from reorganization more limited than commonly believed, but serious obstacles also remain to gauging the contributions that reorganization, or any other change, can make to government efficiency. Despite years of effort, the measurement of government efficiency remains in its infancy. The major stumbling block continues to be the problem of valuing the outputs of government in the absence of a true market. A service delivered from a single state office is certainly likely to be less expensive to provide than the same service delivered through a network of county offices. But it is likely to be worth far less to the recipients. The dilemma is that we rarely know how much less since the costs are not borne by the users through a direct purchase in the marketplace but are shared by all taxpayers. Efficiency, in other words, is a far more complex concept than economy. Economy implies only a reduction in costs. Efficiency implies a relationship between costs and outputs. Conceivably, a reduction in costs can reduce efficiency rather than increase it if the quality or quantity of services declines more than proportionally to the reduction in costs. In the absence of adequate documentation, however, such judgments must rely heavily on guesswork or wishful thinking, undermining much of the rationale on which reorganization for economy and efficiency is based.

A third problem with reorganization for economy and efficiency results from the fact that savings often depend more on programmatic changes than organizational relocations. Locating similar land management agencies in the same department, for example, will not automatically reduce costs either for the federal government or program users if these agencies operate legislatively different programs that remain different after the move. Reorganization must still be followed by legislative program changes if the savings are to be realized. While locating the programs in the same agency may make such programmatic reform more likely, it hardly guarantees it. What is more, programmatic streamlining is occasionally possible without reorganization. Certainly from the point of view of savings in user costs, streamlining and coordination of procedures among closely related programs is as valuable when done across program lines in the absence of reorganization as it is when done within a single agency following reorganization. Preemptive coordination of this sort is, in fact, one of the classic defense mechanisms agencies can employ to fend off the threat of reorganization.

A fourth problem with reorganizing for efficiency and economy arises from the fact that efficiency, for all its appeal, is not a costless goal. Its pursuit sometimes competes with other goals that are more highly valued, at least by some key political actors. That this is so is a product of the major features of American administrative behavior discussed earlier. As noted, the way a program is administered can differ from agency to agency because of differences in agency ethos and in the structure of interests surrounding an agency. Because of the degree of discretion left to program administrators, a shift in agency jurisdiction can therefore alter the basic content of a program. What is more, as Harold Seidman has argued so forcefully: "Organizational arrangements are not neutral. . . . They tend to give some interests, some perspectives more effective access to those with decision-making authority. . . ."[18] An organizational change that contributes to efficiency and economy may thus reduce responsiveness to some interests and viewpoints. For those centrally affected, these consequences may be far more important than the limited savings likely to be possible.

Finally, our knowledge of the real relationship between changes in organizational structure and gains in efficiency is grossly imperfect. The standard nostrums linking savings to the elimination of overlapping and duplication may, in fact, be wide of the mark. Such hypotheses certainly have little credence in traditional economic theory where competition, not monopolization, is viewed as the best guarantee of efficiency. In public organizations as well, economies of scale may be available only up to a certain point, beyond which increased organizational size may lead to increased costs of coordination and communication that ultimately outweigh gains in efficiency.[19] Indeed, even the first Hoover Commission, popularly associated with the bigger-is-better school of management, cautioned against "too much centralization." In its report on federal housekeeping services, for example, the commission pointed out that "in a large scale effort like the Federal government, too high a degree of centralization of services may result merely in congestion, red tape, and inefficiency."[20] The problem is that neither the Hoover Commission nor subsequent work has established the point at which concentration becomes "too high." As a result, there is neither empirical nor theoretical basis for gauging when further enlargements contribute to efficiency or its opposite.

## Reorganizing for Policy Effectiveness

If reorganizations are most commonly defended in terms of economy and efficiency, they are most commonly pursued for reasons of effectiveness.

Effectiveness is a far more abstract and controversial goal, however, than economy and efficiency. Where economy and efficiency focus on the input side of government, on reducing the costs for a given level of output, effectiveness concentrates on the output side, on the question of organizational purposes and the success with which those purposes are met. Where the economy and efficiency argument treats the individual program as the primary unit of analysis, moreover, effectiveness concerns focus more heavily on collections of programs, or policies, as the appropriate unit of analysis.

As is the case with the economy and efficiency school of thought, a wide assortment of specific organizational changes has been associated with the goal of effectiveness. Nevertheless, the explicit doctrine underlying this set of goals is far less well developed than that associated with the economy/efficiency school. This reflects in part the long-standing neglect of organizational purpose in the scholarly literature on organizational behavior[21] and in part the politically inspired emphasis on economy and efficiency as the major goals of reorganization.

Nevertheless, it is possible to discern three key precepts that run through much of the discussion linking reorganization to improved governmental effectiveness. As with most of the other cause-and-effect relationships attributed to reorganization, these three have hardly been articulated explicitly, let alone tested empirically. Yet they form the heart of the rationale that has implicitly informed proposals for federal reorganization for several decades.

The first precept concerns the inadequacies of what Daniel Patrick Moynihan has termed the "program approach" to public problems and the superiority of what Moynihan terms the "policy approach."[22] What differentiates these two approaches is the range and complexity of action and considerations each embraces. Where the program approach focuses on narrowly defined purposes and activities (e.g., the construction of bridges), the policy approach takes greater account of the interrelationships among activities and their implications for broad purposes (e.g., improved transportation). In this view, individual programs can operate efficiently yet prove ineffective in dealing with major national problems because their effects are canceled out by other programs, or because they are too limited in scope to cope with the underlying realities involved.

Reorganization's contribution to governmental effectiveness therefore derives, in this view, from the impetus it can provide to a policy approach to public problems. While there is no illusion that organizational structure is the only factor influencing the extent to which a policy approach is applied to a particular set of problems, it is considered, in this view, to be one of the more important contributing elements, if not a necessary condition. The more programs relevant to a particular problem are scattered organizationally, the more difficult it is to mobilize them in support of a coherent general purpose. The grouping of government programs by major function can thus be defended, from this perspective, less for its contribution to efficiency and economy than for its contribution to governmental effectiveness. Though not widely recognized, this argument was clearly articulated in the report of the first Hoover Commission, long regarded as the bible of the economy and efficiency view of reorganization. In the commission's own words, what was most important about "placing related functions cheek-by-jowl" was not that overlaps would be eliminated and costs reduced, but *"of even greater importance coordinated policies can be developed."*[23] This principle was well illustrated in the commission's recommendations for reorganization of transportation activities, which faulted prevailing arrangements for making it difficult "to think, or act, in terms of total transportation requirements" and which called for "a close grouping of the major transportation activities" not to reduce costs but in order to encourage "the development of intelligent, total transportation policy."[24]

This hypothesized relationship between the grouping of functions by major purpose and the achievement of a more effective policy approach rests not alone on the mechanical ease of coordination that is supposed to result. Of equal or greater importance is the political room for maneuver that such grouping of programs can open. Given that each bureau or agency exists within a narrow "structure of interests," the more isolated the bureau, the more subject it is to narrow, parochial pressures. Grouping of agencies therefore also involves grouping of interests. Out of the resulting competition for influence, political leaders can secure the compromises they need to shape and weld individual programs into coherent policies. Organizing for effectiveness in this sense means arranging the operating units of government in such a way as to achieve enough balance and diversity in the political forces surrounding the major points of decision to permit broad national interests to hold their own against the more narrow, parochial ones embodied in particular programs. "The question," Harold Seidman has noted, "is one of balance. In the design of any political structure, whether it be the Congress or the executive branch, it is important to build in arrangements that weigh the scale in favor of those advocating the national interest."[25] On a more limited scale, reorganizing for effectiveness can mean relocating an agency or program to an institutional environment more supportive of its basic purposes.

A second key precept of reorganization for effectiveness flows directly from this first one. If effectiveness involves fitting programs together into policies that address valid public purposes, it also involves strengthening the role of the Presidency. This view was most clearly articulated in the Report of the Brownlow Committee appointed by President Franklin Roosevelt in 1936. According to the committee, "strong executive leadership is essential to democratic government today."[26] "The plain fact is," President Roosevelt emphasized in his letter transmitting the Brownlow Committee's report to Congress:

> the present organization and equipment of the executive branch of the Government defeats the constitutional intent that there be a single responsible Chief Executive to coordinate and manage the departments and activities in accordance with the laws enacted by the Congress. Under these conditions the Government cannot be thoroughly effective in working, under popular control, for the common good.[27]

This linkage between effective government and presidential administrative authority finds reflection in virtually every major official study of executive branch reorganization. Most significant, perhaps, was its endorsement by the first Hoover Commission in 1949. Though identified frequently with a politically naive set of organizational doctrines aimed at achieving economy and efficiency,[28] the true significance of the first Hoover Commission lay elsewhere. As historian Peri Arnold has observed, the real impact of the Hoover Commission was to "undercut the conservative and congressional opposition to the expansive executive" and provide "the bridge over which the congressional opponents of the Brownlow Committee recommendations and the old political enemies of Franklin Roosevelt could now embrace the managerial Presidency."[29] Rather than point the way back to a more limited view of the role of the Presidency, as hoped by the many conservatives who were buoyed by his appointment to head Truman's postwar Commission on Organization of the Executive Branch of the Government, Herbert Hoover turned on his old allies and endorsed the view, expressed early in his Commission Report, that

> an energetic and unified executive is not a threat to free and responsible government. . . . Strength and unity in an executive make clear who is responsible for faults in administration and thus enable the legislature better to enforce accountability to the people.[30]

This notion that governmental effectiveness depends critically on "the establishment of a responsible and effective chief executive as the center of energy, direction, and administrative management"[31] rests, in turn, on two major arguments, one theoretical and one political. The theoretical argument flows out of the scientific management literature of the early twentieth century, which informed the development of large-scale business organization and which, through Presidents Taft and Hoover, came to dominate the thinking on public administration as well. The central thrust of this literature was a belief in the need for a strictly hierarchical structure of authority, with narrow span of control at each level and adequate staff resources at the top, in order to give direction and ensure accountability in large organizations. As the closest governmental approximation to the chief executive officer of the corporate world, the President was the natural beneficiary of these orthodox administrative principles.

Supplementing this theoretical, administrative-science explanation of the contribution presidential power can make to governmental effectiveness, however, is a political one that stresses the President's unique position as the only public official chosen by a national electorate. The central argument here is that because of this unique position, the President has the greatest incentive and the best political base from which to penetrate the narrow structures of interest surrounding individual bureaus and programs and apply the leverage needed to move them into greater harmony with a broader conception of the public good. With legislative power splintered among numerous committees and subcommittees operating relatively autonomously of one another, the Presidency, in Seidman's words, "stands almost alone as a counterweight to these powerful centrifugal forces."[32] Improving the President's capacity to control the separate parts of the executive branch is thus a means to give precedence to policy over program and general interest over particular interest.

As the opponents of the New Deal recognized, however, the expansion of presidential management control endorsed by the Brownlow Committee and the Hoover Commission is not without substantive content, whatever its patina of scientific legitimacy. The general interest that the Brownlow Committee sought to give President Roosevelt the power to enforce on the Federal establishment was clearly tied to the goals of the New Deal. "A powerful president equipped with the personnel, planning, and fiscal control necessary to implement his social program—this was the Committee's aim," its historian has noted.[33] What this points up is a third key precept of reorganization for effectiveness. Because effectiveness has to do primarily with government purposes, with the appropriate ends of government action, it inevitably raises questions of public philosophy that are more political than scientific in character. The distinction between policy and program discussed earlier does not, after all, describe a sharp dichotomy so much as a continuum. What one person views as an end goal of government activity deserving of institutional expression (e.g., improved housing or transportation) may be viewed by another as merely the means to the achievement of a broader policy goal (e.g., sound urban development). While objective analysis can clarify program interrelationships and guide organizational choices, decisions about which groupings of activities to enshrine in organizational form ultimately depend not on some immutable principle of management but on essentially political judgments about the most important goals of government action. Reorganization, in this view, is an expression of policy, and the calculus of reorganization, in Herbert Kaufman's phrase, "the calculus of politics itself."[34]

What this means in practice is that reorganization for effectiveness involves a continuous tradeoff between two competing concerns. The first is the degree of *salience* to be given a particular subject. By giving organizational expression to a collection of programs or set of concerns, reorganization can increase the likelihood that administrative energies will be focused around the concern, that high-level attention and resources will be devoted to it, and that top-quality personnel can be attracted. In so doing, it can increase the effectiveness with which government addresses the concern.

Because it involves elevating particular functions organizationally and thereby fragmenting governmental structure, however, greater salience runs

73

headlong into a second set of concerns: the need to group activities to ensure *balance* and promote coordination. Conceivably, every major program or activity of government could be enshrined in its own department or agency. However, while the result might enhance *program management* (i.e., the operation of individual programs), it would likely impede effective *policy management* (i.e., the setting of priorities among related programs and the mobilization of individual programs in pursuit of more general goals).

As a rule, reorganizations for policy effectiveness tend to favor balance over salience. This is not to say that separating new organizations out of existing arrangements cannot be justified in terms of improved policy effectiveness. To the contrary, reorganization for effectiveness frequently takes this form. What it does mean is that considerations of effectiveness shift the burden of proof in such cases to those advancing claims for greater salience. Further institutional fragmentation is justifiable, in these terms, only when the function around which a new agency is to be organized is clearly of major importance in its own right, when considerations of timing or the existing distribution of responsibilities make it difficult to pursue the subject effectively or coherently in the absence of a separate institution, and when the gains of separate institutional status clearly outweigh the reduced potential for integration and balance among related activities and interests that is likely to result.

These judgments are naturally not only subjective but also subject to change over time as government assumes new responsibilities and national priorities change. When the first Hoover Commission recommended that transportation functions be grouped together but left within the Department of Commerce, for example, it did so not on narrow management grounds but because it judged that "since transportation is an element in the costs of practically every other industry, Government policies on transportation should be coordinated with Government policies toward industry in general."[35] That this judgment was reversed twenty years later proves not that the Hoover Commission was wrong but that federal priorities and responsibilities had changed in the interim.

Reorganization for effectiveness, in other words, involves a continuous process of weighing the relative merits of balance and salience in organizational design so that administrative structures can be adjusted to national priorities with due regard for the political and institutional dynamics surrounding different programs and agencies at particular points in time. Understandably, such efforts require the most subtle politico-institutional analysis imaginable. The practitioner of reorganization for effectiveness must therefore be a kind of institutional geneticist, skilled in knowing which organizational units to graft to one another in order to create new mutations capable of serving the changing demands on government and the changing priorities of political leaders.

Because of their imputed ties to high-priority policy goals, reorganizations aimed at improved governmental effectiveness are frequently regarded as the only ones worth the effort.[36] But this hardly makes them any easier to achieve. To the contrary, such reorganizations must clear an unusually difficult set of hurdles. In the first place, the very abstractness of the concept of effectiveness makes this form of reorganization hard to defend on its own terms, especially in the face of strident claims on the part of well-placed interests that their bureaucratic preserves are being downgraded and buried in pursuit of it. Greater clarity and precision about the goals of the change hardly offer an antidote, moreover. For one thing, reorganization legislation does not grant authority to alter program purposes and operations. Recognizing this, the congressional committees with jurisdiction over reorganization prudently take care not to appear to cross the imaginary line between reorganizing and legislating lest they alienate the authorization committees whose responsibility it is to set basic program purposes. At a minimum, the price of clarifying the substantive goals of reorganization can therefore be to surrender the important tactical advantages afforded by the use of reorganization, plan authority, and necessitate reliance on formal legislation instead. Beyond this, such clarification can invite criticism from those who differ with the substantive twist reorganization is intended to give to particular programs—who believe, for example, that the goal of the Federal Highway Administration should be to build roads, not serve as part of some vague construct known as multimodal transportation policy, or that the Federal Housing Administration should encourage home construction and not promote "urban development."

The resulting dilemma is nicely illustrated by the fate of the two major departmental reorganization proposals generated by the Carter Reorganization Project in 1978. Eager to counter critics who portrayed reorganization as mindless box shuffling, reorganization planners stressed the policy advantages that would flow from grouping land and water resource programs in an integrated Department of Natural Resources, and community and economic development programs in a Department of Development Assistance. In response, the leadership of the Senate Government Affairs Committee refused to consider the proposals under reorganization authority, arguing that the changes in purpose contemplated in the proposals, while worthwhile, were too significant to accomplish through reorganization authority. Faced with the prospect of a lengthy legislative battle, the administration quickly dropped its plans.

What this experience suggests is that the very dynamics of the reorganization process encourage a conspiracy of silence about the real goals of reorganization. No wonder one scarred veteran of the reorganization wars has concluded that "while a reorganization may come as an incident of material policy change in a specific field, professional reorganizers are well advised to profess neutrality as to substantive goals and insist on the time-honored distinction between administration and policy."[37] In the process, however, reorganizers are deprived of the most important arguments for their proposals, and reorganization proposals are forced to go forward on grounds that are largely specious.

The first set of hurdles to reorganizing for effectiveness would be less telling were it not for a second hurdle related to the way reorganization proposals are generated. To make the most of reorganization as a tool of policy, the generation of reorganization proposals must be closely integrated with the development of policy. As obvious as this observation is, it seems honored more in the breach than in practice. Traditionally, questions of executive organization have been turned over to outside experts operating largely independent of the central policy development processes of the executive branch. Often reorganization comes to be viewed not as a tool of policy but as an alternative to policy, a cheap way to express concern about a subject for which no new resources are available. Worse yet, reorganization can be employed merely as a symbolic balm to generalized citizen displeasure with the perceived unwieldiness of government. As such, reorganization becomes a branch of policy in its own right, utilized for its symbolic value but disembodied from substantive goals, despite what is now known about the dynamics of administrative behavior. During the Carter administration, for example, the effort to link policy and reorganization by housing the reorganization staff in the Office of Management and Budget was largely frustrated because those in control of the central policy development processes in the White House tended to view reorganization as an alternative to substantive policies, not as an instrument of them. Although efforts were made to integrate organizational proposals with the policy objectives that emerged during the formulation of the Carter urban policy, for example, these efforts were largely repelled by those charged with developing the policy, despite widespread acknowledgement that institutional problems were among the most serious impediments to making policy effective.

A third hurdle that must be faced by reorganizations aimed at improving governmental effectiveness involves the difficulty of actually capturing the opportunities for coherent policy that such reorganizations theoretically make possible. The heart of the problem here is that reorganizations can often do little more than convert serious *inter*departmental coordination problems into serious *intra*departmental coordination problems. This is especially true where the political price that must be paid to secure acquiescence in a proposed reorganization is protection for the organizational integrity and autonomy of the agencies affected. Unless departmental management is sufficiently effective in using budgeting and other devices to encourage changes in focus and direction, the results can be rather limited, despite the comforting fiction of a unified departmental structure.

Finally, there is increasing reason to question whether the link between reorganization and government effectiveness, dependent as it is on the notion of dividing governmental functions among cabinet departments, is as strong as it once was. This is so because the validity and utility of departmental divisions have grown increasingly tenuous in recent years in view of the growing complexity of the issues government has been called upon to resolve and the resulting need to mobilize resources and coordinate activities across a broad span of functional areas. Then Budget Director Charles Schultze made this point forcefully more than a decade ago when he told the Senate Committee on Government Operations:

> The answers to our current organizational dilemmas are not to be found in the reports of the two Hoover Commissions and the President's Committee on Administrative Management. The Hoover Commission solution of "placing related functions cheek-by-jowl" . . . is not workable when you must combine major purpose programs such as health, education, manpower training, and housing in alleviating

77

the social and economic ills of a specific metropolitan area, city, or neighborhood.[38]

Only by creating monster departments can such issues be addressed through reorganization, but this can contribute to internal departmental problems every bit as serious, and as cumbersome, as those that now exist across departments. What may be needed, in short, is not simply reorganization but also a more potent set of coordination devices than has yet been developed. Rufus Miles put the issue well recently when he noted: "The most difficult task of public management is not deciding how the functions of government should be effectively coordinated after they have been divided. All government is a complex of matrices: if work is divided on one set of principles or axes, it must be coordinated on another."[39] Since coordination has a reputation even more dreary than that of reorganization, however, the prospects for improved governmental effectiveness are cloudy at best.

### Reorganizing for Tactical Advantage

If reorganization for effectiveness is the most promising but also the most difficult form of reorganization, the third major type of reorganization is the easiest to accomplish but also potentially the most dangerous. This third type consists of reorganizations that are less concerned with economy, efficiency, or effectiveness than with simple political advantage or narrow tactical purposes. In truth, of course, this type is not so much category as a residual, and an impure one at that, since political advantage is involved in virtually every organizational change. Nevertheless, this category is still useful to distinguish two remaining, related types of reorganizations. The first are the large number of reorganizations undertaken primarily for a variety of limited tactical reasons—to downgrade or get rid of an unwelcome official, to secure a change in congressional venue, to bury a program, to change an agency's image, to give the appearance of action, to convey an impression of managerial competence, to pay off a political debt, to forestall more radical change, to remove an agency from the budget or put it on, to shield an activity from congressional scrutiny, or for various other reasons. What these purposes have in common is their rather narrow instrumental character. Taken together, they demonstrate the versatility of reorganization, its utility as a tool for the pursuit of a broad range of tactical, as well as strategic, purposes.

The second major reorganizations included here are those in which the tactical objective sought is primarily political in nature, that is, where reorganization is pursued chiefly to gain access, representation, visibility, and a secure institutional niche for a particular interest. Perhaps the defining characteristic of reorganizations of this type is their tendency to fragment administrative authority rather than concentrate and consolidate it. In the tradeoff between salience and balance discussed above in connection with reorganizing for effectiveness, reorganizations for access and representation shift the presumption to the *salience* side of the equation. Such reorganizations thus have no place in traditional administrational theory, which views fragmentation as a barrier to good management.

Reorganizing for political advantage does find support in democratic theory, however, for the major arguments in its behalf take the form of claims for representation. In this view, political representation cannot afford to stop at the voting booth or the legislative arena; it must penetrate the bureaucracy as well. This is so because the administrative arena has grown too complex and the degree of discretion lodged there too sizable to monitor, let alone control, effectively from the outside. To be represented in government, each interest must be represented within the administrative apparatus. It must have its spokesperson on the inside to express its point of view and look after its interests. What is more, since prestige and power are measured by proximity to the throne, just as in the Court of Louis XIV, each interest must have an institutional home as high in the administrative hierarchy and as close to the President as possible —in the White House if possible, and if not there in the Executive Office of the President, and if not there in a separate agency reporting directly to the President, and so on.

Thus are unleashed a host of centrifugal forces whose avowed intent is to fracture the executive structure, establish visible and well-protected beachheads of power and authority, and thereby insulate particular functions from broader political control. The ultimate purposes to be served by this form of reorganization run the gamut from the purely symbolic to the largely programmatic. Institutional autonomy and organizational elevation are sought to secure status, to enhance budget prospects, to gain access to critical decision channels, to guarantee a steady flow of information, to protect particular professional values, to attract more prestigious personnel, to protect operating programs from interferences or downgrading, and to advance a variety of other pure or impure purposes.

Reorganizations of this sort frequently culminate the rise of new political interests, which seek to signal and solidify their arrival in national politics by acquiring clear institutional form and thus providing themselves with a safety net against any fall from political grace. In justifying elevation of the Housing and Home Finance Agency to cabinet status, for example, Budget Director Kermit Gordon noted that it would "give appropriate recognition to the importance of housing and urban development. . . . It will help to assure that urban needs are given equal consideration with other national needs in the formulation of national development policies."[40] Change the subject and the same formulation could be used for every major reorganization of this type.

While they complicate the task of management and broaden the span of control at each administrative layer from the President on down, reorganizations for access and representation therefore offer a safeguard against majority tyranny, an institutional protection for unpopular functions of government, and a degree of stability in government operations. For these reasons and others, such reorganizations typically enjoy substantial political support, at least from the constituencies that stand to gain from them. Since they constitute a way to satisfy these constituencies without greatly expanding costs—at least in the short run—such reorganizations are also extremely attractive to politicians, including Presidents. Despite campaign rhetoric about the need to streamline government, therefore, reorganization for access and representation continues to be the dominant form of reorganization.

## Conclusions and Implications

Among Washington insiders, reorganization has a reputation very much like that enjoyed by the practice of hitting oneself on the head with a hammer: the only good thing about it is that it feels so good when you stop. All Presidents since 1912, with the exceptions of Wilson and Coolidge, have launched major efforts to reorganize the administrative machinery of the federal government; and according to conventional wisdom, all have in one fashion or another, failed. As a result, reorganization has come to be viewed as a losing proposition, a subject to be taken up when times are calm and substantive distractions few, but to be avoided except in symbolic terms when important matters are at stake.

The discussion here suggests that this conventional wisdom is both conceptually flawed and factually incorrect. If reorganization has failed, it has failed only in terms of a narrow and inappropriate standard, one informed by a simple-minded image of the purposes of the enterprise. In point of fact, the purposes of reorganization go well beyond the narrow confines of economy and efficiency to embrace the purposes of politics itself. Pursuing these purposes through reorganization may be difficult and complex. But if reorganization is a thorny tool of policy, it is also a fairly powerful one. Its target is formally not the content of decisions but the structure through which decisions are reached. Yet, as philosopher Paul Diesing has noted, "Unless a decision structure exists, no reasoning and no decisions are possible."[41] More than that, because in the American context the decision structure importantly shapes the range of interests brought to bear at the point of decision, reorganization ultimately affects the content of decisions as well, not only once but time and time again until the structure is reshaped.

Given the important purposes reorganization has been called upon to serve, it is regrettable that the subject has not attracted more theoretical attention and that the prevailing conceptions remain so imprecise. If we are to understand the phenomenon of reorganization better, it seems clear that progress will be needed in the way we think about it, in the formulation of useful categories to sort out the jumble of facts and provide a basis for meaningful general statements. Although the purposes of any particular reorganization may, like beauty, depend ultimately on the eye of the beholder, it has been the contention of this chapter that theoretical progress in sorting out the long laundry lists of purposes of reorganization is possible. While none of the categories mentioned here may exist in pure form in any particular proposal, the distinctions nevertheless point up important differences in the nature of these proposals and in the political prospects that confront them. Clearly, the typology developed here hardly exhausts the range of distinctions that are possible among the goals of reorganization. If this typology has pointed up the breadth of purposes reorganization can serve, demonstrated the need to categorize these purposes into a manageable number to permit clearer thinking, and begun this process of categorization, it will have amply served its purpose.

NOTES

1. In: U.S. Congress, House, Committee on Government Operations, *Hearings on Reorganization Plan No. 2 of 1977*, 95th Cong., 1st sess., 18 and 21 October 1977, p. 20.
2. Norton Long, "Power and Administration," in Norton Long, *The Polity* (Chicago: Rand McNally, 1962), pp. 50-63. Initially published in *Public Administration Review* 9, no 4 (1949).
3. Ibid., p. 42.
4. In 1975, two-thirds of all career executives had worked in the same agency since achieving GS-13 status. Only 12 percent had worked in three or more agencies since becoming GS-13s (the lowest executive position). As one writer recently put it, career executives effectively have "terms of office" of 17 to 25 years in the same agency. Hugh Heclo, *A Government of Strangers* (Washington, D.C.: Brookings Institution, 1977), pp. 117-18.
5. The discussion here draws heavily on Lester M. Salamon and Gary Wamsley, "The Federal Bureaucracy: Response to Whom?" in Leroy Rieselbach, *The Responsiveness of American Government* (Bloomington: Indiana University Press, 1975).
6. Harold Seidman, *Politics, Position, and Power: The Dynamics of Federal Organization* (New York: Oxford University Press, 1970), pp. 131-32.
7. Harvey Mansfield, "Federal Executive Reorganization: Thirty Years of Experience," *Public Administration Review*, July/August 1969, pp. 333-34.
8. Seidman, *Politics, Position, and Power*, pp. 23-27. Rufus Miles "Considerations for a President Bent on Reorganization," *Public Administration Review*, March/April 1977, pp. 155-59.
9. House, *Hearings on Reorganization Plan No. 2 of 1977*, pp. 37-38.
10. Ibid., p. 33.
11. U.S. Commission on Organization of the Executive Branch of the Government, *Report to the Congress: Department of Agriculture*, Report No. 6, (Washington, D.C.: U.S. Government Printing Office, February 1949), pp. 24-25. Future references to the Commission on Organization of the Executive Branch of the Government will be cited as First Hoover Commission, followed by the relevant report title, number, and page.
12. First Hoover Commission, *General Management of the Executive Branch*, Report No. 1, pp. 34-35.
13. Quoted in Richard Polenberg, *Reorganizing Roosevelt's Government: The Controversy over Executive Reorganization, 1936-1939* (Cambridge, Mass.: Harvard University Press, 1966), pp. 7-8. See also Seidman, *Politics, Position, and Power*, pp. 7-8, 27-28; Miles, "Considerations," p. 162; Mansfield, "Federal Executive Reorganization," p. 334; and Herbert Kaufman, "Reflections on Administrative Reorganization," in *Setting National Priorities* (Washington, D.C.: Brookings Institution, 1977), p. 403.

14. Arthur Holcombe, "Administrative Reorganization in the Federal Government," *Annals of the American Academy of Political and Social Science* 95, (May 1921): 247, quoted in Edward Hobbs, *Executive Reorganization in the National Government* (University, Miss.: University of Mississippi, 1953), pp. 26-27.

15. U.S. Bureau of the Census, *Statistical Abstract of the United States: 1979* (Washington, D.C.: U.S. Government Printing Office, 1979), p. 275.

16. Ibid., p. 275.

17. U.S. Office of Management and Budget, *Reorganization Study of Development Assistance Programs*, December 1978, p. 15, mimeo.

18. Seidman, *Politics, Position, and Power*, p. 14.

19. See, for example, Anthony Downs, *Inside Bureaucracy* (Boston: Little, Brown, 1967), p. 271.

20. First Hoover Commission, *Office of General Services—Supply Activities*, Report No. 3, p. 3.

21. As Frederick Mosher has noted, in much of the literature and research on formal organization, "organization is seen more as a platform upon which human beings may be observed and studied than as a cooperative system for the accomplishment of purposes." Frederick Mosher, "Analytical Commentary," in Frederick Mosher, ed., *Governmental Reorganizations: Cases and Commentary* (Indianapolis: Bobbs-Merrill for the Inter-University Case Program, 1967), p. 484.

22. Daniel Patrick Moynihan, "Policy vs. Program in the 1970s," *The Public Interest*, Summer 1970.

23. First Hoover Commission, *General Management of the Executive Branch*, Report No. 1, p. 34.

24. First Hoover Commission, *Department of Commerce*, Report No. 10, pp. 14-15.

25. Seidman, *Politics, Position, and Power*, p. 303.

26. The President's Committee on Administrative Management, *Report of the Committee, Submitted to the President and the Congress in Accordance with Public Law No. 739*, 74th Cong., 2nd sess. (Washington, D.C.: U.S. Government Printing Office, 1937), p. 53. Cited hereafter as *Brownlow Committee Report*.

27. "Message from the President of the United States," 12 January 1937, in *Brownlow Committee Report*, p. 10.

28. Seidman, *Politics, Position, and Power*, p. 4.

29. Peri E. Arnold, "The First Hoover Commission and the Managerial Presidency," *Journal of Politics* 38 (February 1976): 48-50.

30. First Hoover Commission, *General Management of the Executive Branch*, Report No. 1, pp. 3-4.

31. *Brownlow Committee Report*, p. 3.

32. Seidman, *Politics, Position, and Power*, p. 36.

33. Polenberg, *Reorganizing Roosevelt's Government*, p. 28.
34. Kaufman, "Reflections on Reorganization," p. 406.
35. First Hoover Commission, *Department of Commerce*, Report No. 10, p. 15.
36. Kaufman, "Reflections on Reorganization," p. 406.
37. Mansfield, "Federal Executive Reorganization," p. 334.
38. U.S. Congress, Senate, Committee on Government Operations, *The Federal Role in Urban Affairs; Hearings,* 90th Cong., 1st sess., 28 June 1967, pp. 4261-62.
39. Miles, "Considerations," p. 160.
40. U.S. Congress, House, Committee on Government Operations, *Hearings: Department of Housing and Urban Development,* 89th Cong., 1st sess., April 1965, p. 84.
41. Paul Diesing, *Reason in Society,* quoted in Aaron Wildavsky, *The Politics of the Budgetary Process* (Boston: Little, Brown, 1964), p. 253.

# 5

# The Coordination Option

## ALLEN SCHICK

Allen Schick is a senior specialist in American government and public administration in the Congressional Research Service. He previously served on the staff of the Brookings Institution and as a faculty member at Tufts University. Schick has published numerous articles on planning, programming, and budgeting systems, management by objective, zero-base budgeting, and other efforts at government reform, and has received both the Brownlow and Mosher awards from the American Society for Public Administration. One of the architects of the current Congressional Budget Process, Schick is the author of a recent study of that process, *Congress and Money: Budgeting, Spending and Taxing.*

If reorganization were appraised solely in terms of the transformation of structure—the regrouping of agencies and programs—the record would be disappointing. But much more organizational change occurs than might be discerned from an examination of the structure and location of federal agencies. Perhaps the most prevalent changes are those that seek to improve the coordination of organizationally separated activities.

Coordination is a variegated pursuit. It proceeds through formal lines of authority as well as informal modes of cooperation. Coordination speaks to the relationships between agencies as well as among their constituent parts. Coordination occurs among peers and between superiors and subordinates. Coordination is perceived by some as the essential purpose of organization and by others as an antidote for organizational failures.[1] Coordination can be regarded as a means of, or as a substitute for, reorganization. According to Seidman, "there is probably no word in our

administrative terminology which raises more difficult problems of definition."[2] Yet Seidman offers a useful definition of the process and purpose
of coordination: "the bringing together of diverse elements into a har-
monious relationship in support of common objectives."[3] This definition
encompasses both "weak" and "strong" coordination, arrangements that
merely solicit cooperation from separated organizations and those that rely
on formal procedures for harmonizing different organizations.

## The Need for Coordination

Governments coordinate because they cannot, or do not want to, integrate
their programs into self-contained organizations. At least three explana-
tions can be offered for the failure of the federal government to group its
programs into units that contain all the activities related to a common
purpose. One has to do with the benefits of organizational redundancy,
another with conflict and/or between organizations, and a third with the
lack of consistent or universal criteria for integration.

### Planned or Preferred Redundancy

Separation might be sought because the redundancy provided by it is
valued.[4] A government might set up a multiplicity of intelligence-gathering
agencies because it does not want to be dependent upon a single channel
for information vital to its national security. Or it might invest in redundancy because of a belief that the overall effectiveness of certain programs
would be enhanced. Thus, it might finance a multiplicity of job-training
centers in the same community in the expectation that more hardcore
unemployed would be reached than if a single center were permitted.

Redundancy often is valued because it provides decision makers with a
pluralism of viewpoints and allows for a pluralism of decision makers.
President Franklin Roosevelt was famous for addressing the same issue to
various advisers, thereby expanding the range of options presented to him.
Congressional committees sometimes ask various staff agencies for reports
on the same subject, thereby opening the legislative process to a diversity
of opinions and analyses. In the late 1970s, for example, the Congressional
Budget Office, the General Accounting Office, the Office of Technology
Assessment, and the Congressional Research Service concurrently studied
energy legislation pending before the Congress.

Perfect redundancy—agencies that have identical missions without different capabilities or perspectives—is rare. Even if they start with the same purpose, agencies are likely to specialize in different ways, seeking out their own clients and supporters, and ultimately finding their unique niche in the pantheon of government organizations. As a consequence, once redundancy is established, it cannot be conveniently ended by combining the several units into a homogeneous structure. More would be lost than just the redundant capabilities of duplicative organizations. Because of this, however, those who support the continued operation of separated units might seek to coordinate them. If there are many intelligence agencies, demands are likely to be heard to streamline them into more efficient operations, or to establish a clear chain of command so as to avoid confusion and embarrassment. Only rarely is redundancy so valued that the different units are deliberately walled off from contact with one another. This has sometimes happened in Congress—the most pluralistic institution in American government—with committees instructing staff agencies to conduct research without consulting one another. More frequently, redundancy invites coordination, though not necessarily in an effective or welcomed manner.

## A Pluralism of Interests

The federal government is fractured into a multiplicity of agencies because American politics is splintered among a multiplicity of interests. The standard formula of pluralist politics entitles each important interest to its own programs, agency, and legislative committee (or subcommittee). This arrangement links interest groups, legislators, and agency officials into a mutually advantageous relationship. Interest groups get their own benefits, congressmen their own power centers, bureaucrats their own agencies. The resulting fragmentation is etched into federal assistance, which flows to states and cities through approximately 500 categories; the committee system in Congress, which is divided into more than 300 different units; and the programs of the federal government, which, depending on how they are counted, range from 2000 to more than 10,000 in number. The system is reflected in the organization of the federal government as well. Once the government embarked on substantial involvement in public education in the 1960s, it was only a matter of time until education interests had their own department. The balkanization of the federal organizational structure also is visited upon states and localities through requirements that they designate single agencies to handle various grant programs.

There is no natural limit to the fissions that can occur within the system. Whenever a particular interest gains recognition in its own right, it can aspire to the trappings of pluralist power. Education is no longer recognized in Washington as a homogeneous interest but is fractured into as many special interests as coexist in local school systems and on college campuses. Higher and lower education have their own identities and often go their separate ways; different groups watch over special and professional education; public and private schools have distinct interests. Not surprisingly, the House Committee on Education and Labor has permanent subcommittees for (1) elementary, secondary, and vocational education; (2) postsecondary education; and (3) select education; each with its own jurisdiction and legislation. It will not take long for bureaus organized along similar lines to establish themselves as quasi-autonomous power centers within the Department of Education.

The system is an insular one, with each interest compartmentalized into its own concerns and structures. Insularity is reinforced through the web of advisory groups, professional and trade associations, and newsletters that dot the Washington scene. The term "networking" has become popular as a label for how access and influence work, demands are made upon government and satisfied, and individuals move from staff jobs on the Hill to law firms, lobbies, and high administration posts.

Reorganization cannot fuse the compartments into an integrated structure. After each consolidation drive has run its course, Washington is left with more bureaus, advisory groups, and categorical grants than before. This recurring experience suggests that coordinating mechanisms might be more welcomed than structural reorganization.

Nevertheless, there has to be a perceived need for coordination in order for it to succeed. Affected interests must perceive greater gain in linkage than in isolation; otherwise they are likely to continue on their separate ways. As long as government is sufficiently affluent so that it can satisfy each interest without worrying about the total cost or about the spillover effects on other interests, coordinators will have a difficult time getting the various parties to work together. Interests might unite for logrolling purposes, to pressure for more or to protect one another against outside encroachment. With an affluent society assuring positive-sum outcomes, politics can be practiced as "who gets what," without much concern about who loses. Politics can be organized as a distributive process so that the advantages accruing to some interests are not taken from others. In terms of organizational arrangements, as long as affluence prevails, it would be futile to force discrete interests into marriages of inconvenience. Together in the same organization, they would continue to live apart. Reorganization might create holding companies or conglomerates, but not integrated structures.

Note, however, that compartmentalization depends on affluence. Under conditions of scarcity (real or perceived), interests might be forced to compete against one another for limited resources. Compartmentalization breaks down when politics becomes a redistributive process in which more for one interest means less for another. Thus, states and cities lobby together for higher federal assistance but against one another for division of the spoils. Regions organize into competing groups, each demanding its fair share of the budget. Environmentalists and energy producers lock horns on access to public lands.

Competition forces interests to recognize relationships with adversaries. But scarcity brings its own organizational problem: if it is difficult to merge separate, but compatible, interests into a single organization, it would seem a hopeless task to unite competing interests. Yet some reformers argue for forcing competing interests into the same organization. This line of reasoning led the 1974 Bolling Committee (the Select Committee on Committees) to propose creation of a single committee on energy and the environment in the House:

> The select committee believes it has created a properly balanced committee by combining energy and environment. Energy resources on the public lands are vast and . . . the use of these resources can adversely affect the environment and also require, for coal and oil shale development, very large quantities of scarce water resources. These resource questions and the major questions of environmental policy would be placed in one committee where they can be heard and resolved.[5]

This recommendation was criticized both by exploiters of energy resources and guardians of the environment. Neither party wanted to be locked into incessant combat with the other, and so the House rejected the Bolling proposal and opted instead for a more modest reorganization of its committee structure. Several years later (1977), the Senate reorganized its committees by establishing separate committees for energy and the environment.

If divergent interests cannot be integrated, can they be coordinated? It was suggested earlier that coordination requires the various parties to perceive some advantage in the relationship. If this is so, it might not be feasible to bring discordant interests together even for limited purposes. The task of contemporary coordinators might be to devise new relationships that do not depend on shared interests or symbiotic advantage.

### Lack of Integrating Criteria

Coordination often is sought because no single organization can house all related entities. An organizational structure considered integrative from one perspective might be regarded as disintegrative from a different vantage point. Attempts to integrate the delivery of services in the field can complicate policy coordination at headquarters. An alignment that would weld the intelligence community into a homogeneous organization would undoubtedly sever some vital ties to the armed forces. The reorganization that recently united many education programs in the Department of Education also separated them from child care and Head Start, which remained in HEW (renamed the Department of Health and Human Services). This separation was not merely the result of compromises to win congressional support for the new department but arose from insoluble problems in organizational design. In a complex world, when a multifaceted organization is pulled in one direction, some of its important linkages are weakened.

For this reason, coordinating devices are needed even when reorganizers achieve structural reform. Where only one structure is possible, numerous coordinating links can be built. Indeed, reorganization can be expected to generate more rather than fewer coordinating mechanisms. In the aftermath of the creation of the Department of Education, new coordinating links will have to be built between the new agency and the successor to HEW. Matters that once were handled in-house without formal arrangements now will require formal procedures to compensate for the loss of once easy relationships. One of the problems besetting the Department of Energy in its first years was the need to open bridges to just about every other organization in Washington. The department, which was supposed to integrate energy programs, was paralyzed by the need to coordinate its activities with everybody else's energy-related programs. A similar problem has confronted Congress. Recent attempts to rationalize its committee structure have been accompanied by a steep rise in multiple referrals of legislation to committees. While other factors partly account for this phenomenon, the use of joint and sequential referrals suggests that no single committee structure could satisfy all interested parties.

For this reason, coordinating procedures should be regarded as a means of maintaining the diversities of American political life, not as concessions to failure or as second-best remedies. Coordination speaks to the health, not the pathology, of government. It recognizes the virtues of redundancy, diversity, separateness, and even conflict. The fact that coordinating devices often are weak and transitory by comparison with what might be achieved through successful reorganization should not detract from their utility.

Coordination comes in many forms. Some devices are weak, others are strong. Some rely entirely on voluntary participation, others mandate certain procedures. Some are prescribed by law, others are dictated by Executive Orders. The following sections catalog and analyze some of the principal coordinating alternatives applied in recent years. While this should not be regarded as a complete taxonomy of coordinating alternatives, it covers the main ones.

### Coordination with Information

A common complaint among uncoordinated organizations is that one agency does not know what others active in the same field are doing. "If only we knew," the promise is, "we would be able to avoid overlap and duplication, and we would coordinate our work with theirs."

Catalogs, inventories, source books, data banks, and computerized information systems multiply apace the growth of federal programs and agencies. A few years after Congress doubled the number of legislative staff agencies (from two to four), the Appropriations Committee ordered the development of a research notification system to keep each agency informed of what the others were doing. CRS issues a weekly report on new and completed projects, showing for each the starting and expected (or actual) completion date, the committee or member (by name or category) requesting the research, the name and telephone number of the person directing the project, the product to be issued, other staff agencies (to be) contacted, and a brief description of the project.

Government regulation is an area currently considered in need of reorganization as agencies produce reams of controversial, and sometimes contradictory, regulations. President Carter issued Executive Order 12044 (14 March 1978) providing for the publication of a calendar of federal regulations. The calendar is a schedule of the major rules under development by various regulatory agencies. For each rule, the calendar identifies major related regulations, collaboration between the agency issuing the rule and other agencies as well as with state and local governments, and the sectors affected by the action. Each agency also is required to issue a regulatory agenda specifying its plans for new rules and regulations. There is a good chance that the calendar and agenda will be accorded statutory recognition in regulatory reform legislation working through Congress.

The multiplication of federal assistance programs has spawned efforts to coordinate via information. A stream of OMB directives call for notifying federal, state, local, and regional officials of pending and approved grants. OMB lists federal assistance available to states, localities, and other eligible recipients in its *Catalog of Federal Domestic Assistance,* which is updated semiannually. OMB also maintains the Federal Assistance Program Retrieval Systems (FAPRS), a computerized data bank covering much of the information classified in the Catalog. Apparently all this information is not deemed to be sufficient by Congress, for the Federal Program Information Act of 1977 calls for development of a central source of information about federal assistance.

This was followed a year later by the Federal Grant and Cooperative Agreement Act, which (among other things) provides for a feasibility study of a comprehensive guidance system for federal assistance programs.

Washington has so many information systems that compilation of a full inventory would be a prodigious and perhaps impossible task. Each "compartment" has its own informational network, computerized files, source books, directories, and so on. Indeed, coordination by information has created its own coordination problems. Information overload is so great that the current emphasis is on information systems showing interested parties where to go to get information.

There also is a tremendous yearning for a single system that would put it all together. The 1970 Legislative Reorganization Act directed OMB and the Treasury to develop "for use by all federal agencies, a standardized information and data processing system for budgetary and fiscal data." The Congressional Budget Act of 1974 expanded the scope of this assignment and transferred lead authority to the General Accounting Office for "standardized data processing and information systems for fiscal, budgetary, and program-related data and information . . . to meet the needs of the various branches of the Federal Government and, insofar as practicable, of governments at the State and local level." One of GAO's activities under this mandate has been the development of an inventory of all federal programs. A likely step will be issuance of an official inventory of federal programs.[6]

To what extent has the information blizzard improved program coordination? While no single conclusion could cover all organizational relationships, a number of impressions can be offered.

1. Agencies responsible for issuing informational material often regard the assignment as a chore rather than as an opportunity to coordinate the activities of other agencies. They generally limit themselves to packaging the information submitted by contributing agencies, only rarely undertaking their own data collection. There are exceptions, of course, especially when the lead agency's sole (or principal) function is informational coordination. Thus, the Regulatory Council established by E.O. 12044 has taken its charge very seriously and has worked with participating agencies to improve the regulatory calendars and agendas.

2. Information can lead to formal coordination by identifying overlaps and opportunities for cooperative action, but this is not an inevitable next step. When they testify before Appropriations Committees each year, congressional staff agencies point to the research notification system as evidence of collaboration. They use this argument to rebuff suggestions for a thorough review of the jurisdiction and scope of the various support agencies. In the intergovernmental field, information has served for the past decade as a substitute for overhaul of the grant system.

3. Yet it is also true that information can be a precondition for formal coordination. A logical step before imposing new procedures is to

93

know how various programs and agencies relate to one another. GAO's program inventory has provided a basis for sunset proposals requiring periodic congressional review of all federal programs. Sunset legislation approved by the Senate in 1978 would have prescribed a common termination date for all programs classified within the same category.

4. Information systems introduce their own coordination problems. Not only can the number and variety of informational resources overwhelm and confuse users, it often is difficult to get two or more systems dealing with the same matter to adopt common formats, classifications, and data bases. OMB and Treasury have different rules for reporting on federal assistance; GAO has its own numbers, as does each agency making grants to state and local governments.

5. Agencies resist standardization in data collection. Information is too important for an agency to allow outsiders to dictate what is collected or how it is used. Each agency has its particular needs and traditions and might lose valuable initiative and independence if it abandoned its own system or bowed to standards imposed by outsiders. Information helps agencies justify their missions and budgets. Information provides intelligence on what is happening outside and helps to build ties to an agency's clients. While agencies often are willing to share their information with others, they are unwilling to be dependent on others.

6. For this reason, proposals for a federal statistics or informational czar (or agency) have been vigorously opposed by federal agencies. While opponents speak about invasion of privacy and costs, agency independence is an equally compelling concern. Even if a central information bureau were established, it probably would be unable to coordinate data collection by other agencies. OMB's experience under the Federal Reports Act offers telling evidence. Although OMB has overall management responsibility for the executive branch and has sweeping control over data collection by federal agencies, it has not used its power to significantly shape or constrain agency data collection practices. It bears mentioning that OMB, under pressure from Congress, took over both the *Catalog of Federal Domestic Assistance* and the Federal Assistance Program Retrieval Systems from other agencies that had developed

these systems for their own needs. The 1974 Congressional Budget Act stripped OMB of a lead role in developing a federal program information system because it had dragged its feet in performing the duties assigned by the 1970 legislative reorganization act. As an agency that sees the budget process as its central concern, OMB is not likely to assign high priority to its information chores.

## Peer Coordination

Interagency groups are extensively used to link separated agencies sharing related concerns. Hundreds of commitees and councils with members drawn from a dozen or more agencies operate within the federal government. Some have been established by law, others by Executive Order or administrative action, some have no formal status. These groups operate on a "separate but equal" principle, though in some instances one of the participating agencies may be more equal than the others.

Members of interagency groups send staff representatives—usually subordinate employees—to committee meetings. The assigned staff do not ordinarily develop strong group ties, for their principal mission is to represent the interests of their respective agencies. They never forget where "home" is or that interagency work is only a part-time pursuit. When they circulate and review memoranda and participate in the drafting of reports and recommendations, their job is to make sure that their agency's views are taken into account.

Interagency groups are criticized as ineffective means of coordination. The bill of particulars against them includes charges that they bury rather than resolve problems; that they make it difficult to get things done by opening up the decision process to agencies with only peripheral interests in the matter; and that within a short time after their establishment, participants lose interest in the work.

Yet interagency groups keep on getting established. Just about every President comes into office determined to curb the practice but leaves with new committees authorized by his signature. Jimmy Carter was especially concerned about these groups and viewed their reduction as a key part of his drive to streamline the federal government by cutting the number of federal agencies from 1900 to 200. However, during one twelve-month stretch, Carter issued executive orders establishing (1) an Interagency

Coordinating Council to deal with urban and regional policy; (2) an Energy Coordinating Committee to "ensure that there is communication and coordination among Executive agencies concerning energy policy"; (3) a national Productivity Council to identify "overlapping and duplicative programs which should be eliminated"; (4) a Regulatory Council to "help ensure that regulations are well coordinated"; (5) the Federal Legal Council "to resolve problems in the effective and efficient management of Federal legal resources"; (6) the Management Improvement Council "to improve the effectiveness and responsiveness of Federal programs"; and (7) the Consumer Affairs Council "to improve the management and coordination" of Federal consumer programs.

Harold Seidman has succinctly explained why interagency committees proliferate: nobody has been able "to devise satisfactory substitutes." He regards these groups as "organized ways of promoting voluntary cooperation" and as "useful in setting the metes and bounds of agency jurisdictions and areas of legitimate interest."[7] The plain fact is that no amount of restructuring could create self-contained units, each minding its own business without caring about what other agencies were doing. Boundary and spillover problems are ubiquitous in the federal government because agency jurisdictions cannot be cordoned off from one another. Long before the 1979 embargo on grain shipments to the Soviet Union, foreign policy was recognized as intertwined with the nation's economy and domestic politics. Through highway construction, the Transportation Department has exercised greater sway over urban development than has the department established for this purpose. The welfare system covers housing in HUD, food stamps in USDA, job training in Labor, fuel assistance in the Community Services Administration, medical care, cash grants, and so forth. Energy is everybody's business, including the Department of Energy's.

Because interagency groups are needed does not mean that they are equally effective. The following thoughts are neither comprehensive nor conclusive, but suggest that additional research might yield fresh insights into the role and potential of these groups as coordinating devices.

—The effectiveness of an interagency committee depends less on its formal status than on the extent to which member agencies share common interests and perspectives. The unofficial "Troika" that brought the Budget Bureau, Treasury, and the Council of Economic Advisers together in the 1960s played a greater role in coordinating economic policy than did the succession of economic policy groups established by Executive Order and law in the 1970s. Troika was successful because its members shared much the same outlook about the use of economic knowledge and the ability of the federal government to assure economic growth without inflation. When confidence about economic policy collapsed, the basis for effective coordination was destroyed.

—Interagency committees cannot succeed as organizational orphans. When nobody has a vested interest in the group's work and nobody is responsible for following through on its decisions, a committee will languish even if its formal status remains intact. This problem cannot be overcome merely by arming one of the group's members with "convenor" or "lead" status. The lead agency has to care enough to invest the group with resources and support. A full-time staff often is one of the means by which a committee possesses the ability to sustain its own operations. In order to make this investment, the lead agency normally can be expected to transform the group from a college of equals into an instrument of its own policy. During the heyday in the 1950s, the National Advisory Council on International Monetary and Financial Problems functioned as an arm of the Treasury, which provided staff and guided its work.

Voluntary coordination thus can be more effective than directed coordination, even when the latter emanates from the White House. Coordination of this sort probably is much more prevalent than that which is mandated by outsiders, though it is likely to receive less notice than when it is prescribed by the White House or in a formal pronouncement. There is a simple reason for the favorable prospects of voluntary coordination: the various parties come together of their own accord because they perceive some advantage in coordinating their separated activities.

Yet the frequent recourse to mandated coordination suggests that voluntary arrangements are often deemed inadequate. Lacking formal status or outside direction, voluntary relationships can wither because of declining interest in participating agencies. Plans to get together on a regular basis tend to be preempted by busy schedules or other business. Moreover, peers might prefer directed to voluntary coordination, either because it might give them preferential status (such as "lead" agency designation) or some other advantage vis-à-vis other parties. A final reason for seeking outside direction is to enable an excluded party (e.g., the White House, another agency) to influence the outcome.

The record suggests that interagency units generally have a limited period of usefulness and are most effective when applied to a particular purpose, especially in response to a pending crisis or problem. Over the short run, participants might subordinate some interests (not their truly salient one, however) in order to get on with the job; but over time, they are likely to turn to other matters. Many of the groups established in recent years have indefinite purposes and are not likely to generate much interest.

Interagency groups can strengthen their role by zeroing in on a limited number of "targets of opportunity." One of their chronic problems is that they don't know what they are in business for; another is that they try to do everything. The Regulatory Analysis Review Group process has had some success because it was limited by presidential order to no more than twenty important items a year.

Many interagency committees would benefit from sunset requirements limiting them to a few years unless renewed. Sunset would encourage the President and Congress to review the group's performance and might direct attention to whether the coordinating need for which the group was established still exists and is being met. Sunset probably would not terminate many groups, but it might redirect their work and invest them with fresh support.

—Presidential support can enhance a group's status and effectiveness, but it must be doled out selectively in order to be perceived as genuine. Carter's Regulatory Council has made a mark because the White House has accorded high priority to regulatory reform. But merely nominal support from the presidential office is not likely to carry much value. Although the Federal Regional Councils that operate throughout the United States are headed by presidential appointees, this status has had little impact on their effectiveness.

—Interagency groups should not be organized on the principle that everything is related to everything. Not all boundaries and spillovers are equally important. A unit whose membership and mandate cover the "waterfront" is not likely to develop a useful focus or purpose. A group that effectively links State, Defense, and CIA is apt to generate more cooperation and interest among its members than one open to every agency that impinges on foreign policy. There appears to be a tendency, however, to broaden interagency groups. The 1979 Executive Order continuing the Federal Regional Councils provided for twice as many agency members as Nixon's original order establishing the councils. Carter's Federal Legal Council and Interagency Coordinating Council were each launched with 15 participating agencies; the Energy Coordinating Council started with 23 agencies and was expanded to 25 by Executive Order several months later. Agencies appear more vigilant than ever about external relationships and demand membership, even when only peripheral interests are touched. One possible explanation is that the growth of central staffs allows agencies to monitor activities elsewhere in the government; another is that interest groups now sensitize their agencies to matters that otherwise might be ignored. Whatever the reasons, the sprawl of memberships probably has diminished the utility of interagency groups as coordinating devices.

## Coordination via the Budget Process

The federal budget process is an obvious candidate for use as a coordinating instrument. While interagency groups can debate and advise, the budget process forces issues to decision. The famous Jackson Committee lambasted interagency coordination but could find "no good alternative to reliance on the budget process as a means of reviewing the ongoing activities of the departments and raising periodically for Presidential action issues of effectiveness in actual performance."[8]

However, the conventional routines of budgeting can fragment rather than unify the government's decisional perspective. Budget choices tend to be structured agency by agency, each making its own submission, each with its own channels and lines of communication. Agencies do not ordinarily consult one another when they make budgets; rather, they look inward to their own needs and operations. The lines from the agency to the central budget bureau tend to abide this organizational structure.

Since the 1960s, three types of crosscutting procedures have been introduced into federal budget practice:

1. Redesign of the basic process so as to emphasize interagency and interprogram linkages. Planning-Programming-Budgeting (PPB) in the 1960s, was one such attempt; zero-base budgeting (ZBB) in the 1970s, has some crosscutting features, though quite different from those provided in the earlier reform.
2. Special clearance procedures authorizing one agency to review the

budgets prepared by other agencies. The Special Action Office for Drug Abuse Prevention had this role in the early 1970s; the Director of Central Intelligence currently exercises this power.

3. Linkage of crosscutting policy and management issues to the budget process. Many coordinators have tried to exploit the budget's renowned action-forcing capability, though relatively few have succeeded.

### Crosscutting Budget Processes

In concept and design, PPB was antiorganizational. It was predicated on program structures—not, as has been commonly assumed, in contrast to line items but in opposition to organizational categories. A program, by PPB definition, is a grouping of budgetary elements that does not correspond to organizational lines. In a systems view, a program incorporates all government activities and expenditures contributing to the same objective, regardless of organizational location. To make a budget by program, therefore, is to bypass organizational channels. This characteristic of programs explains why agencies fought so long and hard over program structures. If only informational categories were at stake, agencies would not have cared much whether their activities were grouped into one program or another. But program structures were supposed to be decisional categories, and a government can have only one unique classification for allocating its resources. A program budget, therefore, would have been a coordinating framework by means of which organizationally separated but related elements (whether supportive or competitive) would have their expenditures decided concurrently.

PPB was subversive to organizational life in yet another way. It demanded that agencies examine the effectiveness of their activities, seemingly a reasonable expectation but one that would have required them to reach out beyond their own operations to gather data about external conditions. No agency could appraise its effectiveness merely by knowing itself. Moreover, PPB brought cadres of analysts—persons whose first loyalty was to their data and discipline—into government. Unlike managers who were responsible for getting things done, analysts had no function other than to question what their agency was doing. In the end, PPB withered as an organizational misfit.

In isolated instances, agencies embraced PPB for the outreach capability it offered. Mosher and Harr have chronicled the State Department's efforts to use PPB to gain control over other foreign affairs agencies.[9] Significantly, State was opposed by the Bureau of the Budget, which feared that a program-structured PPB system would impair its lines of communications to individual agencies.

Zero-base budgeting, by contrast, is intended to fit into the organization. While it seems to threaten organizations by purporting to examine budgets from a zero base, ZBB actually builds incrementalism into the process. The changes made via ZBB are those recommended by program managers. It prefers the subjectivity of the manager to the objectivity of the analyst because it knows that programs cannot succeed without organizational support. ZBB has generated little of the strain and opposition that afflicted PPB because it does not try to force changes on the organizations using it.

By structuring budget choice agency by agency and within each agency by its administrative subdivisions, ZBB would seem to be a fragmenting rather than a coordinative influence. Yet the 1981 budget credits ZBB with "several interagency reviews [which] have resulted in more integrated, systematic examination of programs with similar or related objectives."[10] Interviews with a number of agency officials provides some support for this claim. ZBB offers a mechanistic but relatively dispassionate procedure for ranking budget requests within or across organizations. Interagency rankings can be made without reaching to the purpose or values of programs. It is much harder to get excited about whether an item should rank twelfth or fourteenth on a list than whether it is worth conducting. Of course, this is a limited form of coordination, but at least it enables the budget process to transcend organization lines.

### Coordinated Review

The usual budget route takes an agency's request directly to OMB without any intervening review. P.L. 92-255 deviated from this pattern by authorizing a new Special Action Office for Drug Abuse Prevention (SAODAP) "to review and . . . modify insofar as they pertain to Federal drug abuse prevention functions . . . the budget requests of any Federal department or agency." SAODAP was placed in the Executive Office of the President and given a clear mandate to coordinate the policies and activities of the more than dozen federal agencies involved in drug-abuse control. In 1975, when the original legislation expired, the Special Action Office was replaced by an agency that lacked its special budget powers. At hearings on the renewal legislation, it was clear that federal drug-abuse agencies welcomed the Executive Office access provided by SAODAP, but not its budget review. One witness argued that "while there is not now nor was there ever any need for SAO to attempt to manage the internal affairs of the agencies it coordinated, there is still great need for some sort of super agency at the highest possible level to work through the bureaucracy."[11] However, none of the many witnesses complained about the results of the special budget review. Most agencies had experienced rising budgets for drug-abuse programs, and there was no evidence that the Special Action Office had seriously constrained their activities.

Executive Order 12036, dealing with the intelligence community, is another instance of coordinated budget review. It gives the Director of Central Intelligence "full and exclusive authority for approval of the National Foreign Intelligence Program submitted to the President." The director has a permanent resource management staff that reviews the budgets prepared by each intelligence agency and packages them into a unified submission. The staff utilizes ZBB's ranking procedures to prioritize agency submissions and to pressure them to reorder priorities with respect to a limited number of items.

In budgeting, as in other organizational processes, the power to review is not the power to command. It provides opportunities to bargain and to influence. SAODAP and DCI were able to bring their particular perspectives to the budget process and try to persuade agencies to redirect some of their efforts. The final outcome was marginally different from what it might otherwise have been. It should be noted, however, that much budget choice is at the margins, a little more or a little less, so that in terms of the degrees of discretion available to the budget makers the small differences might have mattered a great deal.

### Piggybacking the Budget Process

The most extensively used coordinating procedure in budgeting might also be the least effective. Because the budget process is reputed to "force action," it is tempting to link to it weak processes or interests which might otherwise be ignored. The history of the Bureau of the Budget from its placement in the Executive Office of the President (1939) until its termination by reorganization (1970) was of a succession of management concerns assigned to it in the hope that they would gain importance from association with the bureau's budget power. Most were placed in the management side of the bureau, though occasionally they were assigned to the examination staffs. This practice was amplified when the Office of Management and Budget was established. Indeed, a key reason for transforming the bureau into OMB was to emphasize its management role.

But coordination, like planning and evaluation, is a weak process. Each is weak even when undertaken by an agency for its own purposes, because there is no immediate penalty for failure. And they are not strengthened merely by proximity to the budget routines. Budgeting is a process that continues on its appointed rounds regardless of the new interests pressing for attention. OMB examiners are experts at subverting a highly touted initiative by indifference. The President might announce that the budget process will be used to appraise the urban impacts of federal programs or coordinate federal civil rights activities, but these moves will quickly fade away unless they can penetrate to the routines of budgeting. If the President demonstrates sufficient staying power, he might get Budget's attention; without it, the announcement will be a "one-day wonder." This has been the fate of most coordinating initiatives entrusted to OMB.

### Coordination in the Field and in the President's Office

Peer coordination relies on agency-to-agency contacts, usually among central staffs headquartered in Washington. These interagency relationships might not have much impact, however, on what happens in the field. While central officials interact, field officials can continue on their separate paths. Moreover, although interagency contact might protect the boundary and spillover interests of participating organizations, the integrative concerns of the White House might be ignored. Indeed, agencies might be willing to make their own deals in order to avoid presidential involvement in their affairs.

The first of these problems has spurred efforts to coordinate in the field matters that remain organizationally separated in Washington; the second has generated attempts to use presidential power to coordinate matters kept apart by the agencies. Field and presidential coordination concentrate on opposite ends of the organization chart, but often with common objectives.

## Field Coordination

Since World War II, there has been a quiet organizational revolution in Washington. Operating units have been relocated to field offices while their slots have been filled by central staffs (the navy is an exception; it still deploys thousands of operating personnel in the Capitol area). The personnel experts, budget officials, information specialists, planners, analysts, and other central staffs devote much of their attention to monitoring and controlling field operations. The internal reporting systems of many federal agencies have been designed to provide headquarters with extensive information on what is happening in the field.

However, improvements in intraagency coordination can complicate interagency relationships. As field offices become more responsive to guidance from their home offices, they might become less attentive to what their peers in other agencies are doing. This problem is especially serious in intergovernmental programs, most of which have their own funding sources, administrative requirements, and organizational channels. A categorical network that effectively links functional specialists in the field to functional bureaus in Washington can thwart the general interests of the federal agency responsible for the program or the government receiving the federal assistance. States and cities have found it difficult to develop coordinated approaches to their problems when they have to deal with many federal agencies (or with separate bureaus in the same agency) in order to put together a complete package.

Reorganization can offer only limited relief. If federal departments were realigned according to functions (one of the principal objectives of reorganizers), they still would have the problem of dealing with one another, and with recipient governments, in the field. Thirty years ago, James Fesler convincingly argued in *Area and Administration* that there is no perfect or permanent formula for coordinating field and function. Governments face "a choice of adjusting area to function or adjusting function to area," and Fesler urged them "to develop practical compromises."[12] Over the past thirty years, many compromises have been tried, and many more can be expected in the future.

One of the first was the establishment of federal executive boards in cities with a concentration of federal agencies. These interagency groups demonstrated that weak coordination devices are apt to be even less effective in the field than in Washington. Federal agencies are willing to give the executive boards free rein over administrative chores that nobody else wanted to handle, but not involvement in policy matters. The boards kept busy allocating parking spaces and mobilizing federal participation in the local united fund campaign, but they had little to do with programs.

A stronger dose of interagency field coordination was provided by the ten Federal Regional Councils established in 1969. This move was accompanied by the designation of coterminous boundaries and common regional headquarter cities for various federal agencies. The FRCs have had some success in handling short-term assignments such as the federal response to natural disasters and the development of pilot programs. States and cities have found it difficult to develop coordinated approaches to their problems when they have to deal with many federal agencies (or with separate bureaus in the same agency) in order to put testing coordination in the field. The Advisory Commission on Intergovernmental Relations concluded in 1978 that although the FRCs "have engaged in a variety of useful special projects and provided important communications links,"

> they, as yet, have made only minor contributions to the coordination of federal program operations and the strengthening of relations among the levels of government. The most significant constraint upon their activities is the continuing centralization of decision making for many assistance programs and the lack of full administrative authority among the regional officials who make up the council membership.[13]

If ACIR saw the problem in terms of Washington's failure to confer genuine authority upon field officials, Washington's remedy was to vest coordinating authority in state and local officials. Federal agencies thought that it would be easier to change the way states and cities organized themselves for intergovernmental purposes than to change their own operations. This attitude was buoyed by the realization that federal programs had had a good deal to do with the impairment of the power of mayors and governors to effectively manage their governments. Accordingly, "capacity building" was the distinctive coordinating approach of the 1970s; in practice, it meant giving chief executives more say over federal funds flowing into their governments.

OMB's Circular A-85 called for federal consultation with chief executives of state and local governments before the issuance of regulations affecting their jurisdictions. OMB's A-95 provided for notification of state, local, areawide (usually substate regional organizations) units of applications for federal assistance, with opportunity for review and comment before they are approved. A-95's greatest success appears to have been in encouraging planning and coordination by areawide regional councils. ACIR's overall verdict is "that governors and local chief executives have not taken advantage of the opportunities." ACIR doubts "whether the procedure can work effectively as long as primary responsibility for compliance is left with the federal agencies."[14] But another explanation is that mayors and governors have incentives to battle with the functional bureaucrats in their own governments. A chief executive enters the fray after federal funds have been solicited, and vigorous intervention might impede the flow of federal dollars to their jurisdictions. All the nation's mayors and all the nation's governors might not be able to put the humpty-dumpty of federal programs together again.

During more optimistic times, federal officials thought that local executives would be able to coordinate if they had "glue" money to buy cooperation from functional bureaucrats. This approach undergirded the Model Cities program, which provided designated cities with federal funds to plan a coordinated attack on the problems of selected neighborhoods. Having developed coordinated programs, the eligible cities would then receive action grants that would be combined with categorical funds to implement their plans.

The proper epitaph of Model Cities is that it spurred a great deal of planning but not much action. One cannot be certain whether the real problem was that federal money began to dry up before Model Cities could demonstrate its potential or whether its ambitious scope doomed it to disappointment from the start. At any rate, Model Cities was eventually folded into community development block grants, which gave mayors what they really wanted: more flexible use of federal money, not just the headaches of coordinating recalcitrant agencies. But community development's flexibility came at a price, for its scope was narrowed principally to physical and economic development. Model Cities' noble attempt to integrate social services with bricks and mortar programs was abandoned.

After more than a decade of efforts to improve the coordination of intergovernmental programs, ACIR concluded that nothing short of reorganization—the consolidation of grant programs—would work:

> . . . given the aid system as presently constituted, the Commission believes that no independent Presidential, departmental, or even joint Congressional-Presidential efforts on the management front alone can be effective. The ACIR, in effect, adopts the position that no management improvements per se will succeed unless a simultaneous drive is mounted to bring somewhat greater clarity, more balance to the current federal aid system.[15]

ACIR has urged Congress to give the President the same power to consolidate grant programs that he now has to reorganize federal agencies. But if reorganization is any guide, even if a President were given consolidation authority, the coordination problems of the intergovernmental system would not all be solved. There still would be a need for field coordination, as difficult as it may be.

## Presidential Coordination

Until recently, the prevailing view was that the President should be significantly involved in the coordination of federal programs and agencies. Indeed, many observers defined coordination as essentially a presidential role, something that could not be done as well anywhere else in the federal government. Thus, the Heineman task force saw an urgent need for presidential intervention in intergovernmental and interagency matters and urged the formation of a program coordination staff in the White House. These coordinators would serve as "eyes and ears" for the President and as "paratroopers" dispatched to trouble spots for short-term assignments. The Ash Council saw coordination as one of a congeries of tasks to be located in the new Office of Management and Budget. It viewed coordination as an activity that would benefit from association with OMB's other management functions—the budget process, personnel development, information systems, and so on.

These views were consonant with generally accepted principles about the role and place of the President in the organization of things. The modern President, as defined by the Brownlow Committee, was supposed to be the manager in charge of the federal government. Rather than allowing agencies to run matters as they wished, the federal government was deemed in need of the President's guidance and perspective. Of course he needed help, as the Brownlow group succinctly put it, and he got help in the form of assistants placed in the White House and staffs placed in the Executive Office. The former would attend to the political role of the President, the latter to the institutional needs of the Presidency. The President never fully realized the managerial and governing expectations thrust upon him, though the "textbook" model long served as a guide for reorganizers of government and defenders of presidential power.

Two problems were never satisfactorily resolved in determining the managerial reach of the White House. First, how could presidential intervention be reconciled with agency responsibility for its own performance and agency strivings for independence? Second, could the President intervene without damaging his own record, and in a way that would provide for effective implementation of his policies? The first problem led the Heineman group to grasp for departmental organizations that would enable cabinet members to function more as presidential aides and less as captives of their own agencies. Influenced by McNamara's reputed success in the Pentagon, the Heineman task force wanted department heads who would be sufficiently powerful to override the parochial emissaries to their agencies rather than the other way about. In his "plot that failed," Richard Nixon tried to carry this concept a big step further by designating "supersecretaries" with dual roles as agency heads and presidential advisers. The plot would almost certainly have failed even if the Nixon administration had not been ruined by Watergate.[16]

The second problem is how to assure effective White House intervention without overburdening the President. The standard solution has been to give him a sufficient number of aides to watch out for his interests and follow through on his instructions. But these workload remedies generate fresh problems, for an overextended President can be drawn into no-win political situations in which he promises more than he can deliver.

Short of a retreat by the United States in world affairs and by the federal government in domestic matters, the President will continue to be the dominant actor in American politics and will continue to want an effective, institutionalized Presidency. This means that presidential staffs are likely to be large, active, and interventionist in the future. While it might be possible to combine staff discipline (such as prevailed under Eisenhower) with staff activism under subsequent Presidents, my own hunch is that it will be difficult to restrain big staffs from trying to get involved in program operations and that, consequently, the White House will continue to be part of the coordination problem.

No-win situations are likely to be the very issues for which coordination is deemed to be most needed. Conventional wisdom (circa 1970) was that when agencies have competing interests, the President should decide between them and make his decision stick. When federal agencies complicate the conduct of state and local government, mayors and governors should have a direct line to the White House to get the problems cleared up. When several agencies (or programs) must be synchronized in order to achieve a national objective, the President should be the one knocking heads together.

Calls for presidential intervention still are heard, but less compellingly than a decade ago. The American Bar Association's Commission on Law and Economy argued in a carefully developed 1978 report that "one of the central tasks of modern domestic government is to make wise, balancing choices among courses of action that pursue one or more . . . conflicting or competing objectives." The commission found, however, that individual agencies as a whole could not make balancing choices because

> of their principal characteristics: independence, single-mindedness, and multiplicity. These attributes of the modern American regulatory agency are no accident. It is fair to say that in an era when the problems of government were less complex and interdependent, we planned it that way.[17]

The commission regarded the President as "the elected official most capable of making the needed balancing decisions as critical issues arise," and it therefore recommended that he be permitted to intervene in matters "of major significance both to the national interest and to the achievement of statutory goals other than the goal primarily entrusted to the regulatory agency in question."[18]

Although these recommendations were directed at regulatory agencies, they could be generalized to government as a whole. The problem, however, is that a President who concentrates on conflict situations is apt to lack the ability to routinely produce his desired outcomes, no matter how many functionaries are placed under his command.

Much contemporary writing speaks to the limitations of presidential power. From his vantage point as a former department head, Robert C. Wood castigated presidential intervention as more damaging than beneficial to governmental competence:

> The longer one examines the awesome burdens and limited resources of those who help the president from within his immediate circle, the more skeptical one becomes of a strategy for overseeing government by "running" it from 1600 Pennsylvania Avenue.[19]

Wood's views have been voiced by a growing chorus of political scientists. Richard Rose came away from an examination of Nixon's management-by-objectives system doubting whether a President has many real objectives and convinced that "an Administration's policy in a given area—if the policy is to be an achievement rather than a mere aspiration— must normally be carried out" through the agencies which "have their hands on the personnel and resources that constitute the outputs of government."[20]

By the time Jimmy Carter took office, the new wisdom was that a President should intervene less and allow the agencies to manage more. Stephen Hess advised Carter in a book released shortly before his election to rely on his "Cabinet officers as the principal source of advice and hold them personally accountable . . . for the operation of different segments of government."[21] Carter has reportedly heeded this advice: the most management-oriented President of recent times has been more disengaged from managing the government than were any of his recent predecessors.

I sense that we are on the brink of a more balanced conception of the modern Presidency. Neither the "imperial" nor the "collegial" Presidency offers a satisfactory model. Presidents cannot always be sideliners in order to stay out of trouble or intervenors trying to get their will done. There is a place for selective intervention by the President, and this will require not only a balanced view of the reach and limitations of the White

House but also reliance on coordination schemes that do not engage it, and perhaps some structural reorganization as well.

## Conclusion

Governments coordinate because they cannot (or do not want to) integrate. The reorganization route often is closed off by opposition from agencies and interests which fear that they would lose power and status, and by uncertainty over the consequences of structural change. Through Carter has been an exception, the White House has generally been reluctant to invest much political effort to overcome the resisters and doubters. Yet some structural changes are worth fighting for; some structural defects can thwart even the best coordination schemes. Coordination and reorganization often are interdependent. When the White House believes that an organization's structure is deficient because it separates matters that should be joined, it might think in terms of a combination of structural and coordinative remedies.

Coordinative alternatives are likely to be more effective for developing than for implementing policy. This explains why the remedies sought for improving the "delivery" of Great Society programs failed to accomplish even the modest objectives set for them. Delivery requires command of the attention and resources of the organization in charge of getting things done. The basic routines of administrative management have to be applied to the task, along with enough staying power to see the effort through to completion. The fleeting interest of interagency groups, peer coordinators, or chief executives cannot suffice.

When it is measured against the possibilities of structural reform, coordination often seems to be a feeble, wasted endeavor. Coordination appears to be weak and unstable, time-consuming and exhausting. It doesn't change the power relationships among agencies and therefore cannot overcome organizational impediments to effective management. Coordination, we are forever being told, cannot get agencies to do things against their own interests.

Why then is coordination so frequently tried? The cynical response is that coordination is a way of showing action when none is really wanted. I would not deny the critics their ample evidence but would urge another explanation. Coordination is a means of reconciling the interests of a pluralistic political system with the realities of an interdependent society. It is futile to guage the effectiveness of coordination in terms of what integration might accomplish. When structural integration is beyond reach, governments would do well to explore the possibilities of coordination.

## NOTES

1. Mooney defined coordination as "the determining principle of organization, the form which contains all other principles, the beginning and the end of all organized effort. James D. Mooney, "The Principles of Organization," in Luther Gulick and L. Urwick, *Papers on the Science of Administration* (New York: Institute of Public Administration, 1937), p. 93.
2. Harold Seidman, *Politics, Position, and Power* (2d. ed.; New York: Oxford University Press, 1975), p. 195.
3. Ibid.
4. See Martin Landau, "Redundancy, Rationality, and the Problem of Duplication and Overlap, *Public Administration Review* 29 (1969): 346-58.
5. U.S. Congress, House Select Committee on Committees, H. Rept. No. 93-916, part 2, p. 37.
6. Sunset legislation being considered in the 96th Congress would provide for an official inventory of all federal programs. See H.R. 5858 and S. 2.
7. Seidman, *Politics, Position, and Power*, p. 203.
8. U.S. Congress, Senate Committee on Government Operations, Subcommittee on National Policy Machinery, *Organizing for National Security* 3:22.
9. See Frederick C. Mosher and John E. Harr, *Programming Systems and Foreign Affairs Leadership* (New York: Oxford University Press: 1970).
10. The Budget of the United States Government, Fiscal Year 1981, Special Analyses, p. 347.
11. U.S. Congress, Senate Committtee on Labor and Public Welfare, Subcommittee on Alcoholism and Narcotics, *Hearings on Drug Abuse Prevention and Treatment Legislation,* 94th Cong., 1st sess., 1975, p. 262.
12. James W. Fesler, *Area and Administration* (University, Ala.: Alabama University Press, 1949), p. 15.
13. Advisory Commission on Intergovernmental Relations, *The Intergovernmental Grant System: Summary and Concluding Observations,* June 1978, p. 7.
14. Ibid., p. 8.
15. Ibid., p. 74.

16. See Richard P. Nathan, *The Plot That Failed: Nixon and the Administrative Presidency* (New York: Wiley, 1975).

17. American Bar Association, Commission on Law and the Economy, *Federal Regulation: Roads to Reform,* Exposure Draft, August 1978, p. 94.

18. Ibid., p. 99.

19. Robert C. Wood, "When Government Works," *The Public Interest,* No. 18 (Winter 1970): 45.

20. Richard Rose, *Managing Presidential Objectives* (New York: Free Press, 1976), p. 160.

21. Stephen Hess, *Organizing the Presidency* (Washington, D.C.: Brookings Institution, 1976), p. 154.

# 6

## Reorganization: When and How?

### I. M. DESTLER

I. M. (Mac) Destler is a senior associate at the Carnegie Endowment for International Peace and director of its project on Executive-Congressional Relations in Foreign Policy. He has served as a senior fellow at the Brookings Institution, a visiting lecturer at Princeton's Woodrow Wilson School, and a consultant on reorganization to the Johnson and Carter administrations. Destler is the author of *Presidents, Bureaucrats, and Foreign Policy: The Politics of Organizational Reform, Making Foreign Economic Policy,* and numerous articles on U.S. foreign policy making and organization.

A new President is elected. Or a new cabinet member or agency head is appointed. He (or she) sees reorganization as a promising means of promoting any one of a number of possible goals: changing substantive priorities, improving responsiveness to executive leadership, conforming to the executive's preferred operating style, or improving program efficiency and effectiveness. How should he proceed? What lessons does postwar experience offer him?

This essay addresses four related tactical questions about the practice of reorganization: (1) When? (2) How broadly? (3) How openly? (4) How to staff?

### When?

"As a general rule, I believe a new President, in the areas where he wants to effect change, must do so within the first four months. He need not complete it within this time, but he must give enough of a shake to the bureaucracy to indicate that he wants a new direction and he must be brutal enough to demonstrate that he means it." Henry Kissinger was speaking in early 1968, about Vietnam policy. But these words have since been aptly cited as predicting the national security reorganization Kissinger set in motion, at Nixon's behest, before the latter was even inaugurated.

More recently, Secretary of Health, Education, and Welfare Joseph Califano moved immediately to restructure the department he inherited in 1977. By March of that year, he announced major steps at consolidation, including creation of a new Health Care Financing Administration; and in July, he ordered reorganization of HEW regional offices. By contrast, President Carter, who campaigned on a reorganization platform, did not move immediately to deliver on this promise—with the important exception of his proposal to create a Department of Energy. Instead he inaugurated a wide range of studies, with submission of reorganization plans deferred until particular investigations were complete.

One of the strongest arguments for immediate reorganization is that stressed by Kissinger. It sends a strong signal—that a new person is in charge, is determined to use his authority, and wants things changed a certain specific way. In the period immediately after a new chief is designated, his subordinates-to-be are in a state of anxious waiting—wondering what he will do, who he will work with and through, what his priorities will be. They are more likely then to respond flexibly to reorganization, it can be argued, than if it comes after a year or two of his tenure, by which time there will have emerged fixed, perhaps even comfortable, new patterns of doing agency business under his leadership. At the beginning, they will see the situation as more fluid.

It will be more fluid to the new executive as well, since he will have a minimum of encumbering prior commitments to people, to policies, or to procedures. Had President Carter decided how he wanted to manage economic policy decisions before he selected his senior advisory team, for example, the Economic Policy Group he established might not have lacked both the preeminent cabinet official and the well-placed staff coordinator necessary to its effective functioning. And in July 1977, to take another example, Carter tentatively accepted the proposal of his reorganization staff that he transfer the Council on Environmental Quality from his Executive Office to the Department of the Interior as part of a broader streamlining of the EOP. The members of the Council objected. They cited his commitment (explicit or implied) to them upon their appointment several months earlier that they were to be, at least in form, *his* advisers. Carter (responding also of course to environmentalist pressures) reversed himself. Had the President moved earlier, before choosing the new CEQ members, he would have been free of one important constraint—their personal claims on him. More generally, the 1977 EOP reorganization came just at the time when senior White House aides were getting themselves established, each with a fresh presidential mandate. It is hardly surprising that no such aide was displaced by the EOP project's results.

There is one final argument for immediate reorganization: the opening of his tenure may be one of those rare times that an executive looks at his responsibilities in a comprehensive way. Thereafter he is likely to become enmeshed in the specifics of policy and operations. It is striking, for example, that books on Nixon administration foreign policy dwell on organizational and procedural changes in opening chapters treating how it all began, but virtually ignore the subject when they move to later months and years. This seems to be a good reflection of what the key actors were stressing—after the first month they were too busy dealing with Vietnam or China to focus on the overall policy-making system they directed.

If there are good reasons for moving right away, there are also strong arguments for caution. One of the most powerful is ignorance; most new executives simply won't know that much about their new jobs, their new institutions, the people with whom they will work, their policy priorities. President-elect John Kennedy told John Kenneth Galbraith in December 1960: "I must make the appointments now; a year hence I will know who I really want to appoint." He would also, he could have added, know more about the organizations they would head, the policies he wanted them to press, and the procedures he found productive and congenial. Thus the recurrent theme of Richard Neustadt's transition memo to Kennedy was that of moving with caution: take no irrevocable decisions until you develop a feel for what sorts of people *you* need, what works for *you*, what fits *your* style.

The point about style deserves elaboration, for often new executives will not really know what their modus operandi will be until they experience it. When Nixon was Vice-President, one of his valued policy experiences was participation in the regular meetings of Eisenhower's National Security Council, for this gave him access to issues from which he might otherwise be excluded. Presumably he was sincere, therefore, when he declared upon the campaign trail his determination to "restore the National Security Council to its preeminent role in national security planning" and announced just after his inauguration that it would be "the principal forum for the consideration of policy issues" requiring his decision. But then he found that as President he didn't like the NSC at all; he preferred the very "catch-as-catch-can talkfests" that he had denounced under Kennedy and Johnson. So the frequency of NSC meetings declined, to the lowest level since the National Security Act of 1947, and Nixon (together with Kissinger) was widely regarded as having consciously perpetrated a fraud.

Speaking more generally, new executives are likely to be, at best, uncertain of their organizational goals and limited in their capacity to relate means to them. They may well either exaggerate or misunderstand what formal changes can be expected to achieve. They may not yet have decided what policies they prefer or—perhaps more important—what policies are politically viable. Thus Eisenhower recounts his advice to President-elect Kennedy on defense:

> I did urge him to avoid any reorganization until he himself could become well acquainted with the problem. (Incidentally, I made this same suggestion with respect to the White House staff, the National Security Council, and the Pentagon.) I told him that improvements could undoubtedly be made in the Pentagon and the command organization, but I also made it clear that the present organization and the improved functioning of the establishment had, during the past eight years, been brought about by patient study and long and drawn out negotiations with the Congress and the Armed Services.[1]

At least one further consideration may argue for waiting. Unless he has had previous experience in his agency, the executive who moves immediately will almost of necessity do so with his own newly assembled team of aides. And this team will be selected, almost certainly, for personal loyalty to the executive or agreement with his organizational or policy goals —*not* for experience or understanding with reference to the organization he comes to head or to its constituencies. This was how Califano proceeded, and it was how his one-time mentor, Secretary of Defense Robert McNamara, proceeded in 1961 when he imposed far-reaching procedural changes on the Pentagon budget process. In both cases, career bureaucrats and their institutions responded as if to a semialien invasion, and the conquest was, at best, incomplete. To quote the conclusion of one careful recent critique of the McNamara regime, which finds its budgetary outcomes "substantially indistinguishable" from those in the Eisenhower administration:

> . . . the behavior of McNamara and his colleagues appears paradoxical in retrospect. Their concentration on restructuring the formal budgeting system suggests an appreciation of the opportunities to exploit the resource allocation process as an instrument of policy and as a mechanism of organizational control. The actual operation of PPBS in McNamara's Pentagon, however, suggests an insensitivity to, if not innocence of, the organizational processes which create the gulf between good decisions and subsequent actions: the administration's dependence on the military services for political support and policy implementation often was disregarded; the officers' incentives seemingly were ignored; and the military's bargaining advantages were strengthened. The administration then struggled to overwhelm or circumvent the resulting opposition with bargaining resources which its own actions had dissipated.[2]

If some time had been devoted to learning about real-life organizational processes in the Pentagon, it might have been worth the wait.

What *criteria* should executives apply in deciding whether to move now or later? Three suggest themselves. The one following most directly from the above is how much the executive knows—about government generally, about being an executive, about the people, the policy area, and the organization with which he will deal. In this sense, the case for fast action is stronger for a Califano than for most others, since he came to his post with impressive prior experience.

A second criterion is how strong the executive's political base is at the outset of his tenure, and whether it seems likely to improve or deteriorate. Since reorganization is likely, at least in the short run, to be a drain on political resources, it would seem logical to undertake it when the supply of these resources is at its maximum level.

Finally, he can consider how long he expects his tenure to be. If it is likely to be just a year or two, then he will have to move quickly or not at all. If he plans to remain a long time, he can better afford to bide his time.

## How Broadly?

How comprehensive should a reorganization be? Should a new executive seek thoroughgoing change, spanning the entire organization he heads, or should he proceed selectively?

Comprehensive restructuring sends a large message: there is intended to be a fundamental new way of doing business. When AID (or the World Bank) shifts from a predominantly functional to a predominantly regional organizational structure, this signals that the country (India) rather than the functional program (agricultural development) is to be the primary basis for program planning and resource allocation. Or if, in an agency long boasting a trim "line" organization, the executive establishes a cross-cutting oversight staff, this indicates clearly that the decisions of line subordinates are to be subject to second-guessing and challenge.

Thus a comprehensive approach is logical when the reorganization goal is system wide. If the objective is to transform cabinet members from special-interest pleaders to broad-portfolio presidential advisers, then a consolidation program like Nixon's "new American revolution" is an appropriate means. If the goal is to revolutionize the way agencies prepare and justify their budgets, then a reform like Carter's zero-base budgeting (ZBB) must logically be implemented on a government-wide scale. (But this need not happen all at once. Charles Schultze's repeated recommendation that the Johnson administration's Programming-Planning-Budgeting-System [PPBS] be introduced gradually looks wise in retrospect. But his President repeatedly overruled him. The result was a change that initially *appeared* impressive, but may have ended up less so.)

Two more specialized sets of circumstances would seem to make comprehensive approaches more attractive, in cases where they apply. One is the existence of entrenched barons in an organization—bureau chiefs whose tenure typically outlasts that of the political executive who ostensibly directs them. The replacement of any one individually is tantamount to personal humiliation, if indeed it is legally or politically possible. It may be more attainable—or more palatable—if it is part of some broader scheme or rationale. Another organizational circumstance suggesting comprehensive reform is the existence of functionally interdependent subunits or programs: if change in one inevitably spills over substantially into another, then it becomes logical to tackle the entire system.

A partial, piecemeal approach can also be the logical response to particular organizational goals. President Carter, for example, entered office with a reorganization commitment but without a developed program or any guiding rationale that had clear operational implications, other than the quickly abandoned plan to reduce the number of separate entities from 1900 or so to 200. The goal became, in practice, to generate a respectable amount of visible organizational change, preferably change that would not be vetoed on Capitol Hill. In this goal his administration has been successful; none of the major reorganization proposals actually submitted by Carter has failed to win congressional acceptance. This is in striking contrast to Nixon's more ambitious "revolution," which never came close to congressional enactment, or to Kennedy's stream of plans to reshape the regulatory agencies according to the philosophy of adviser James Landis. Several of the Kennedy plans were rejected.

These examples demonstrate an important reason for piecemeal change: modest alterations generate far less political resistance than comprehensive efforts. The latter are likely to require taking on a range of constituencies simultaneously, unless their politics is managed with enormous sensitivity and adroitness.

There is another important general case for small steps—the fact that our ability to predict the consequences of large-scale change remains poor. If the bad reputation of the Department of Energy is justified, this may be in part because, inevitably, large reorganizations have countless unintended consequences. There are just too many variables that influence what new patterns of policy making develop, how interest-group access and congressional dealings are altered, and so forth. Advocates of major change tend to assume, at least for polemical purposes, that their goals will actually become operative once their formal fix is adopted. Calls for a new Department of Trade, for example, have this flavor. The safer option is to build on institutions and processes that already work, reinforcing their areas of strength, as the Carter administration ultimately did (for the most part) in its buttressing of the Office of the U.S. (formerly "Special") Trade Representative, which had already established a strong record in government-wide trade policy leadership and coordination.

A piecemeal, step-by-step approach may be appropriate under certain circumstances even if the ultimate goal is broad. If the organization is one like the State Department, where the average tenure in a particular job is relatively short, then changes in bureaucratic structure or particular offices' responsibilities can be timed to coincide with normal personnel transfers, or the timing of these transfers can be marginally adjusted.

If organizational units or programs are functionally autonomous, then it will also make tactical sense to reorganize them one at a time, each according to its own particular needs.

What criteria, then, can officials apply to determine whether to proceed comprehensively or selectively? Four have already been cited: the goal of the reorganization, the personnel fluidity of the bureaucracy involved, the degree of interdependence among programs or units, and the political capital that executives can invest in reorganization. A fifth, which affects how much of the latter is required, is the breadth of recognition in relevant portions of our society that there is some large problem requiring action. Creation of the Department of Defense, and successive restructurings therein, were possible because of recognition that service autonomy was obsolete for much military planning and war fighting. Gasoline shortages, rising fuel costs, and newspaper headlines made a Department of Energy politically attainable in 1977.

## How Openly?

When Lyndon Johnson proposed, in his 1967 State of the Union address, the merger of Commerce and Labor into a new Department of Business and Labor, perhaps twenty people in the United States had advance notice. The President's motives in maintaining such secrecy were no doubt multiple —he wanted to stun people; he feared that if the idea were exposed before he was clearly committed to it vested interests would unite to overwhelm it. But the example suggests several reasons why secrecy is often considered a valuable and even indispensable reorganization tool by those who employ it.

Most obviously, secrecy gives reorganization proponents time—to refine their plans, to develop the best case possible for them—while simultaneously depriving potential opponents of time to build their resistance. Thus it may seem the most practical approach when important interests inside or outside the organization are opposed to the change and cannot be plausibly won over. Had George Meany known well in advance of Johnson's plan, he would have mobilized his forces to block such elimination of "labor's voice in the Cabinet." Indeed, his organizational position would have compelled him to do so whatever his personal views. By maintaining confidentiality and then unveiling the proposal with fanfare, Johnson at least gave it a head start against its critics.

Another argument for closed reorganization planning is that it facilitates analysis undiluted by bargaining. Staff aides can concentrate on developing their options and arguments without the simultaneous need to compromise with critics or affected barons, avoiding the muddy consensus language acceptable to people with varying interests and goals.

But the Johnson proposal failed abysmally once it became public; important interests opposed it, and hardly anybody understood it except a handful of insiders and specialists. Congress never gave it serious attention. This suggests several reasons for more open procedures—like those pursued, for the most part, under the Carter program. Consultation and debate can generate understanding of what the problems are, and what the rationale of a particular reform may be; it can help bring key constituencies on board as active supporters, or at least help them reach the point where they might acquiesce. They can, more generally, give those planning reorganization a clearer sense of the real political world in which their schemes must ultimately be tested. And it may even be possible to energize those within the organization as creators and supporters of change, as proponents of the "organizational development" school of management would argue. Moreover, complete secrecy may be impossible to maintain; and one effect of the attempt at confidentiality may be that only negative reports—partial, misleading, threatening—make their way to the officials affected, increasing their resistance. Simultaneously, secrecy may mean a failure to mobilize constituencies that would support a change. Thus, while Budget Bureau practice until the late 1940s was to maintain almost total confidentiality until a reorganization plan was issued, broader consultation became the norm thereafter.

In practice, the question will often be not whether to consult but when. In most cases, it is probably a mistake to do so before there is a serious proposal (or at least serious options) to discuss, for this may simply stir up anxieties. In other words, there should be something to consult about.

What criteria can then suggest whether openness or secrecy is most fruitful, or what would be the appropriate mix? One question is how much the top executive can personally control the outcome—how much his decision will stick, at least formally. If assent is required from the Congress, for example, the utility of executive secrecy seems markedly reduced, though it could offer short-run tactical advantages in some circumstances. A separate but related question is how self-enforcing the formal reorganization action will be in and of itself. A change in the age limit for entering the foreign service, for example, or in the general structure of the foreign service examination, should prove relatively self-enforcing. If, on the other hand, the decision is to change the assignment sequences of foreign service officers, its execution will require the supportive participation of personnel office specialists responsible for placing particular officers in particular jobs.

Finally, there is the practical question whether persuasion is a practical option or whether authoritative action is required to overcome inevitable resistance. If a change is something an agency will view as contrary to its interests—removing its exclusive control of overseas cable communications, for example—it will have to be ordered. In such cases, secrecy may be useful in making it possible for the executive to decree a change, to generate a fait accompli, before resistance has a change to develop.

## How to Staff?

The preceding pages have assumed that the executive already has a reorganization program, or at least knows the general directions in which he wants to move. Often this is not true. Or he may have certain predilections but want them tested and/or refined. Or he may want them legitimized. He certainly will need them to be put in operational form, with legal and practical issues checked and resolved, action documents drafted, perhaps political bases touched as well.

On whom should he rely to accomplish these things? Executives have in practice employed a range of devices including

1. A publicly established, visible commission to make organizational recommendations: the Hoover and Murphy commissions, the Wriston and Herter committees

2. A senior advisory panel similar to the above, but invisible to the public: the Heineman task force
3. A semipermanent reorganization staff, reporting to one of the executive's senior aides: the President's Reorganization Project of the Carter administration
4. The policy official or officials who are charged with making the system work: Nixon's or Carter's national security staff
5. The career staff of the agency being reorganized: the 1967 Budget Bureau self-study, the Macomber program of "reform from within" at the State Department in 1970

## The Public Commission

One very well established means of reorganizing is to create a visible panel of expert individuals, for a limited term, with a prestigious title, charged with making a public report on organizational problems and changes to remedy them. Such a body can be chosen solely by the executive—like the Secretary of State's Public Committee on Personnel (Wriston Committee) created by Secretary of State John Foster Dulles in March 1954. Or it can be jointly appointed by the President and Congress, like the Hoover and Murphy commissions. Generally, such a commission recruits a staff, holds hearings, carries out some sort of research program, and presents a public report. Its mandate may be government-wide (Hoover), broad within its subject (Murphy), or relatively narrow (Wriston). Its leeway within its substantive mandate can also vary widely. And lest one think this an old-fashioned approach to the subject, let it be noted that on 31 January 1980, Congressman Richard Bolling introduced legislation to establish a "Commission on More Effective Government" that would "consider and study the organization, operation, and functioning of the Federal Government in all of its aspects."

The public existence of an established, expert body tends to legitimize particular organizational changes by giving them the weight of its expert authority. Thus, such a commission can play an important role in sharing with the executive some of the political heat, as Wriston, for example, clearly did. Such a body also provides a counterweight to the agencies, and the senior officials, which reorganization will affect, thus increasing the ability of the staff serving the commission to develop an independent analysis and get that analysis to the executive. Thus, such a commission can improve the chances that the executive will not be served up a set of precompromised choices for him to ratify.

With this political weight, however, comes potential encumbrance, for the visibility and prestige of such a commission reduces the flexibility of the executive on whether he will accept or reject its recommendations. If he appoints responsive people and gives them clear signals, he may limit this problem by controlling, or strongly influencing, what it actually recommends. But the very fact that a commission is public generates pressure, at the outset, for its membership to be made representative of a range of interests and viewpoints. If the group develops considerable prestige and independence, and the executive then does not accept its recommendations, this makes him vulnerable to criticism. And from the executive's point of view, the more visible a commission is, the more likely it may be to develop momentum of its own. Or a public commission can become a sort of political orphan, as the constituencies that supported its creation abandon it and move on to other causes. The Murphy Commission, for example, was originally a Senate Foreign Relations Committee initiative, attached as a rider to the State Department authorization act of 1972. It was initiated as a means to get a handle on the process, and perhaps at least marginally the substance, of Nixon-Kissinger foreign policy making. During most of the commission's life, however, Kissinger was Secretary of State and therefore congressionally accountable, and Foreign Relations Chairman Fulbright was defending him against Senator Jackson's assaults. By 1975, when the commission made its recommendations, the market for them had largely vanished.

## The Private Senior Advisory Panel

An executive may seek the advantages of a senior panel without the public costs, by creating an "inside" senior group, composed of current senior officials or outsiders or a combination thereof, to make recommendations to him alone. The classic example of this approach was Lyndon Johnson's establishment of the President's Task Force on Government Organization (Heineman task force) in 1966, which was, incidentally, one of a number of inside task forces working on various issues that were put together by staff aide Califano. So secret was the Heineman group's existence that when this author was invited to join its staff, he was explicitly told not to discuss his new job with his then current Capitol Hill employer. And the task force's existence was not, to my knowledge, ever noted in public print until well after its work was complete. A variation of this model was Nixon's Ash Council, whose existence was publicly announced but whose reports were for the private use of the President and such aides as he designated.

Such an approach has substantial advantages for the executive if the political culture of the time will permit it, and if he can, without the inducement of publicity, attract the caliber of people he seeks. He doesn't get the reinforcement of his reorganization program that can come from a publicly prestigious panel, but such a group can serve as an effective internal counterweight to the officials and agencies affected, and threatened by, reorganization. Such a panel and its staff, moreover, can operate quite efficiently. Absent public pressures or inquiries, with affected bureaucrats having but limited access to its work, the panel can assign its staff to topics of its choosing, develop serious options unbuffeted by premature political exposure or the necessity to bargain about their language. In choosing the panel itself, the executive has almost total leeway. And he maximizes the chance that he will get an independent product responsive to his guidelines, since the group has no other immediate market. Finally, its recommendations will put him under no immediate pressure to act; Lyndon Johnson apparently concurred in many of the Heineman task force recommendations, and set them aside for priority action in 1969!

The limitations of this approach are the converse of its strengths. No constituencies for change are built, no understanding of organizational problems or the purposes of reorganization is created among those who might suddenly be called upon to implement major structural change. Because analysis and prescription must be closely held, this approach runs a serious risk of ignoring important information or misconstruing the nature of problems or the likely effect of solutions. This tendency is furthered by the fact that the staff must be selected for loyalty to the executive and to the task force rather than experience with the agencies that are candidates for reorganization. Such a panel will almost certainly underrate political constraints. And large formal fixes may be excessively attractive to such a group. Nixon's "new American revolution" proposal, for example, had its origin in a short think-piece report prepared for a general conceptualization of the desirable future structure of the federal government. This was ostensibly not to be a basis for current action but it became the point of departure for an Ash Council report, which was.

### An Ongoing Reorganization Staff

An executive may eschew establishment of a senior commission or panel to buttress (or encumber) him on organizational matters. Instead he may create a permanent or quasi-permanent staff group to work full-time on reorganization issues, a group reporting not directly to him but to his senior management aide. This was the basic Carter administration approach—establishment of the President's Reorganization Project in OMB, with a staff of more than two hundred at its peak. Its job was to conduct studies ordered or authorized by the President, to broker reorganization issues, and to press the development of practical proposals. The work of the staff had formal access to the executive, but through a senior aide—the director of OMB—for whom its particular initiatives and interests were unlikely to be top priority. In organizational location, therefore, PRP was similar to the Budget Bureau's Office of Management and Organization headed by Harold Seidman in the 1960s. But PRP was larger, more visible, and much less experienced; and being recruited specifically for the Carter program, it lacked institutional memory.

This is not a particularly strong way to staff reorganization, and it depends substantially on the caliber and commitment of the OMB director for whatever strength it does possess. But this very fact may offer the President several advantages. He is not encumbered by it, since it lacks the visibility and seniority to cause him major public trouble if he decides against it. And the staff's limited base and generalized mandate forces it to reach out for consensus, to collaborate with affected agencies and seek allies in these agencies, to test the waters on Capitol Hill, to come up with proposals that have good prospects for acceptance by those most closely affected. Indeed, a recommendation strongly resisted by these constituencies has great difficulty, under this system, making its way from such a staff to the President in actionable form.

This method of staffing reorganization will not serve the executive well, however, if he wants strong options that might be perceived as threatening by senior administration officials. For it tends, in practice, to give them a veto power over such options. This problem was particularly acute in the EOP study, conducted by an ad hoc staff buried in the EOP, operating with no direct personal guidance from the President, and supervised by an advisory committee of senior presidential aides known fondly on the staff as the oxes to be (or not to be) gored. One predictable result was a negotiated settlement on the problem of how to allocate cuts in White House staff slots. There were no serious challenges to even those senior White House officials and offices known to be personally distant from the President and his own work. The chance for some real streamlining, therefore, was missed. And the project's very modest impact on OMB came only after the President himself chastised Director Bert Lance about how little affected his own agency was by the study group's proposals, a result of the fact that Lance had overruled the group on certain proposed transfers from OMB after hearing an eleventh hour appeal from those affected. The point here is not that Lance should necessarily have supported the study group recommendations; it is that the system kept them from getting to the President when he did not support them.

An ongoing staff is not necessarily an *alternative* to a senior panel but may coexist with one and support its work. Thus in the 1950s the ongoing Budget Bureau staff supported the President's Advisory Committee on Government Organization appointed by Eisenhower and chaired by Nelson Rockefeller.

## The Responsible Officials Themselves

On 2 December 1968, when announcing the appointment of his new Assistant for National Security Affairs, Richard Nixon noted that "Dr. Kissinger has set up what I believe, or is setting up at the present time, a very exciting new procedure for seeing to it that the next President of the United States does not hear just what he wants to hear." This announcement was premature, but Kissinger did move quickly on this task. Drawing on staff work by two aides, Morton Halperin and Lawrence Eagleburger, and after consultation with General Andrew Goodpaster, he sent Nixon on 27 December a rather substantial memo proposing a detailed structure for the system Nixon had ordered, one centering national security policy making in the White House. Despite strong State Department resistance, Nixon approved the memo, and Kissinger put the system into operation beginning on Inauguration Day.

For the immediate purpose of getting quick action in the desired directions, this method could hardly be improved upon. And the fact that the new system buttressed Kissinger's authority meant, reciprocally, that his evident sponsorship buttressed the system. The main weakness of this approach, at least in this case, was the resentment generated elsewhere, sowing the seeds for later State Department resistance to the Nixon-Kissinger regime. This was in part due to Nixon's refusal to state personally and directly to Secretary of State William P. Rogers that he, the President, was personally committed to this system and rejected Rogers' counterproposals. Thus the new procedures could be seen at Foggy Bottom as not entirely legitimate, as something that Kissinger had foisted on Nixon, as well as on State.

## The Staff of the Affected Agency

Finally, reorganization proposals can be developed by a staff group or groups composed of members of the agency whose restructuring is contemplated. In 1967, partly in response to the work of the Heineman task force, the Bureau of the Budget inaugurated an internal self-study to provide "a critical analysis of its responsiveness and its effectiveness in serving the President and the executive departments and agencies." And in 1970, responding to widespread criticism of his department, Deputy Undersecretary of State William Macomber launched with considerable fanfare, a "Program for the Seventies", featuring thirteen studies by internal task forces, aimed at proving that the department could indeed accomplish "reform from within." In both cases, those who analyzed and reported on particular organizational problems were not the agency operators with day-to-day responsibility for them. But they were careerists with ties to the agency and commitment to its future success.

The potential advantages of such an approach are considerable. It engages in the process individuals with considerable expertise and institutional sensitivity, and with strong personal commitment to their organizations. They encourage among officials a constructive self-criticism and engagement in change (McGregor's "Theory Y"), as contrasted with the defensive, protective reaction that externally conducted studies often generate. And this willingness to generate internal reform can, in fact, be trumpeted as a positive value, lending legitimacy to the reform process by demonstrating that the organization is alive if not entirely well. Thus a contemporary headline in *Government Executive* magazine: *State Department Answers Fulbright*: *"We Can Clean Our Own House."*

129

One important problem with this approach is that the perceptions and interests of those within may not lead to improved responsiveness to constituencies outside. Both Budget and State were under criticism, for example, for inadequate and declining responsiveness to presidential needs. But agency insiders were hardly in the best place to comprehend these needs. Moreover, internal studies inevitably tend not to tread too hard on the interests of careerists, at least when the time comes for action. At least three Macomber task forces, for example, called for "more extensive use of lateral entry as a means of infusing new blood" in the foreign service, but the steps announced as implementation of the studies added up to an actual reduction in the trickle of professionals entering the service at above the bottom ranks. Finally, reform from within does not necessarily mean that individuals personally engaged in the problems under study will be doing the recommending; in fact, one serious limitation in the implementation of the Macomber proposals was that, for people in the State Department personnel office, it was "reform from without": an effort by officials, perhaps well meaning, who had little experience in personnel problems and did not understand the complexities of what they were suggesting. But this moves the discussion to the matter of implementation, the subject of chapter 8.

## NOTES

1. Dwight D. Eisenhower, *Waging Peace* (New York: Doubleday, 1965), p. 713, quoted in Morton H. Halperin, *Bureaucratic Politics and Foreign Policy* (Washington, D.C.: Brookings Institution, 1974), p. 283.
2. Arnold Kanter, *Defense Politics: A Budgetary Perspective* (Chicago: University of Chicago Press, 1979), p. 122.

# 7

# General Propositions of Organizational Design

## ALAN L. DEAN

Alan L. Dean is chairman of the Board of Trustees of the National Academy of Public Administration and a member of the President's Council on Management Improvement. Mr. Dean was formerly Assistant Secretary of the Department of Transportation and has held senior administrative posts in many other U.S. agencies, including the Federal Aviation Agency, the Office of Management and Budget, the Department of Health, Education, and Welfare, and the U.S. Railway Association. He is the holder of several awards for exceptional service. He has participated in the design and management of reorganizations in the fields of public works, space, aviation and transportation, and served as coordinator of President Nixon's Departmental Reorganization Program.

Many of the early writers in the field of organization and management strove to identify and articulate "principles" on which those who were charged with establishing or directing public or private organizations might rely.[1] In more recent years a number of students of management have challenged the validity of such commonly cited "principles" as those relating to span of control, the assignment of authority, supervision, and decentralization. Harvey Sherman in *It All Depends*,[2] pursuasively argues that the often invoked management "principles" are little more than proverbs and that in any event they fail to provide answers to many of the problems faced by today's managers.

This chapter does not seek to reopen the debate over the existence or usefulness of general principles of organization. More words on this subject are not needed and would contribute little to the objective of developing a compendium of useful experience concerning what works or does not work in the organization and management of government agencies.

If, however, we limit ourselves to the organization and management of the departments and agencies of the executive branch of the government of the United States, it is my belief that we can identify and set forth a number of *propositions* that may have general applicability. We should avoid describing these propositions as "principles," for they often more resemble admonitions that should be taken into account in designing organizations, but may not always be controlling.

There is no doubt in my mind that long exposure to the management of government agencies can equip one with a sharpened capacity to predict the success of various approaches to organization when they are applied to known situations. Such an experienced person can design structures capable of coping with new or changed conditions of management with a greater prospect of success than can one who has not acquired such a background. The task of this chapter is to identify the knowledge that underlies these skills and determine if some part of it can be articulated as propositions useful to managers, especially those who have not had the opportunity by trial and error to develop a basis for reliable judgments in coping with problems of organizational design.

It is important to understand that we are dealing with a specific and limited administrative environment. We are concerned only with departments and agencies of the executive branch of the federal government. This is an environment influenced by the Constitution, the Presidency, the courts, the Congress, a body of laws and traditions, a civil service, and a vocal and organized citizenry. What works or does not work in this setting may operate differently in a local government, in a private concern, or in a parliamentary democracy.

In 1947, when I was an organization and management analyst in the Bureau of the Budget, I was asked to review and summarize all proposals for the improvement of the organization of the executive branch that had been developed and published since 1900. This research was performed to assist the bureau in its support of work of the first Commission on Organization of the Executive Branch of Government (Hoover Commission).*

* This twelve member commission, chaired by former President Herbert Hoover produced a number of important reports in 1948-1949 which became the basis of major reorganization proposals. Many were successfully implemented.

It was noteworthy that each of these pre-1947 studies accompanied its findings and recommendations with assertions that were often given the trapping of principles or generally applicable rules. The many post-1947 studies and writings in the field of government organization, including the two Hoover commissions, the Heineman and Price task forces of the Johnson administration, President Nixon's Council on Government Organization (Ash Council), and the reports supporting the President's Departmental Reorganization Program of 1971-72, to list but a few, are replete with advice as to how the executive branch and its counterparts should be structured and managed. The propositions presented here will draw upon the "principles" propounded in the various study reports, but to a greater degree they reflect my direct involvement in numerous reorganizations and agency management improvement efforts over more than thirty years.

It should also be noted that in our system a President or agency head may encounter great difficulty in gaining acceptance of his organizational proposals, even when he clearly understands what should be done. As Harold Seidman so well documents in his *Politics, Position, and Power,*[3] organization affects the distribution of power, and there are many forces arrayed to seek to preserve arrangements that they feel to be in their interests. It is not rare for the Congress, as the result of the impact of concerned interest groups, to reject structures that persons experienced in government administration regard as highly desirable. Often long overdue reforms such as the establishment of a Department of Natural Resources will be deferred or abandoned because the forces arrayed in defense of the status quo are perceived to be too strong to overcome.* Even when a proposed organization is compatible with the propositions discussed herein and wins general acceptance, there may be compromises or limitations imposed resulting from the forces that are at work on the Congress. An example is the refusal of the House of Representatives in 1966 to include the Maritime Administration in the new Department of Transportation, in spite of the fact that the legislation creating the department was well received and was swiftly approved. The Administration bill and the Senate

---

* As happened in 1979 when President Carter decided not to proceed with a Department of Natural Resources proposal after two years of staff work. President Johnson abandoned planning for a Department of Business and Labor in 1966 in the face of strong opposition from organized labor.

version both provided for this transportation unit of the Department of Commerce to be a part of the Department of Transportation.

1. *Effective organizational design is best assured by basing structure primarily on the functions to be performed.* Organization is not, or at least should not be, an end in itself. It is simply a device to help direct the efforts of staff and to deploy resources so as to carry out some function of government. Making this statement does not imply that all the departments or agencies of the executive branch have in fact been designed to perform their current missions most effectively. If one were today to establish an organization to administer the federal government's water resources and river basin functions, it would be unthinkable that the largest programs associated with this activity would be placed in the Department of Defense to be carried out by the Corps of Engineers of the Department of the Army. This anomalous arrangement goes back to the time when the federal government's engineers were West Point graduates, and there was a need to keep them busy in peacetime. The perpetuation of the Corps of Engineers' role in civil water resources matters has constituted a major barrier to the development of a Department of Natural Resources and has imposed heavy burdens of review and coordination on the Executive Office of the President.

There is often a temptation to organize around people, especially a talented head of an agency. Although this can be done at the lower levels of an organization with little permanent damage and some short-term benefits, the consequences at higher levels are usually undesirable. The eventual departure of the official whose abilities have led to the skewing of the organization removes the initial advantages and confronts the President or the concerned agency head with a subsequent need to upset established relationships.

The confusion over the respective roles of the Department of Defense versus the Federal Aviation Agency in the development of the supersonic transport in the 1964-65 period is an instance in which the President entrusted to a Secretary of Defense in whom he had great confidence an oversight role over a project for which the FAA has statutory responsibility and the most direct concern in terms of its civil aviation mission.

The placement of the National Oceanic and Atmospheric Administration (NOAA) in the Department of Commerce instead of the more logical Department of the Interior is another instance of a presidential decision based on a preference for one cabinet Secretary over another. In this case, Commerce Secretary Maurice Stans had the confidence of the President, while Interior Secretary Hickel was not well regarded by the White House.

In summary, reliance on existing agency capacity or the talent of particular officials may seem to justify organizational actions that subordinate functional considerations, but in the long run damage will be done to the programs involved and the ability of the executive branch to assure effective management.

2. *Agencies concerned with the execution of government programs should be established to reflect the purposes sought by those programs.* This proposition is so phrased as to exclude agencies with a staff or service function, such as the components of the Executive Office of the President, the Office of Personnel Management, or the General Services Administration. It does apply to the executive departments and all independent agencies charged with carrying out programs that involve government services to the citizens, either directly or through grants or other forms of assistance to state and local governments.

To some it may appear that this proposition is obvious and that there is no other way to organize. Such is not the case. For many years there have been departments and independent agencies proposed or actually established for reasons that relegated the purposes of the programs involved to a secondary role in the determination of structure and the assignment of functions.

For example, in 1938 President Roosevelt established by reorganization plan a Federal Works Agency and a Federal Loan Agency. These agencies reflected recommendations of the President's Committee on Administrative Management (Brownlow Committee),[4] and they were based on the processes involved or the type of work to be performed. These reorganizations produced such strange combinations as the placement in the Federal Works Agency of the Bureau of Public Roads and the Public Building Administration. Both the FWA and FLA failed to meet the needs of the executive branch, and after a few years they were abolished with few mourners. Now most construction and financial assistance programs are administered by the departments and agencies whose major purposes they support. Federal highway functions are thus carried out in the Department of Transportation, and federal public buildings responsibilities are discharged by a housekeeping agency, the General Services Administration.

Yet we still hear proposals for new executive departments lacking an identifiable purpose, such as a Department of Science. In theory the research and technological functions now supporting the various departments could be combined with the National Aeronautics and Space Administration and National Science Foundation in a department that could be described as scientific in terms of the primary professional occupations of its staff. Wisely, no President has endorsed such a department, nor have the various bills providing for such an agency made much progress in the Congress. It is now the preponderant view that scientific programs are as vital to the support of major purposes as are financial assistance programs or construction activities and, therefore, should remain in the departments whose missions they facilitate.

A number of the extant executive agencies, such as the Department of Labor, have been oriented more to serve a clientele than advance a broad major purpose. For years leaders of organized labor have viewed the Department of Labor as providing a spokesman in the cabinet for the interests of labor. Some secretaries and principal officials of the Department of Labor have in the past accepted this as their role. This "clientele" approach to departmental and agency organization has stood in the way of restructuring the executive branch by major governmental purposes. Clientele departments have not been noted for their effectiveness either in developing policies or administering programs, and they have often been charged with failing to consider the broad public interest.

President Nixon attempted in 1971 to restructure the executive branch along major-purpose lines when he proposed the abolition of seven domestic departments and their regrouping into four departments concerned respectively with community development, human resources, national resources, and economic affairs.[5] While none of these departments became law, for reasons too involved to discuss in this chapter, the idea of organizing the executive branch into a smaller number of departments arranged around the central purposes of government was widely supported in principle in the congressional hearings of 1971 and 1972.

It can be asserted as a corollary to the proposition under discussion that the more we consolidate related programs into large departments or agencies concerned with broad major purposes, to that extent we will strengthen the capacity of the executive branch to meet the increasingly difficult task of administering the multitude of programs now carried out by the government of the United States.

3. *Programs contributing directly to a definable major purpose of the federal government should be placed within the same department or agency.* In my judgment the application of this proposition should be an important objective in the effort to improve effectiveness in the delivery of public services. In virtually every instance in the last forty years in which an organizational change has been consistent with this proposition, important benefits have been realized and can be documented.

As with all the propositions set forth in this chapter, there will be those who will challenge the validity of the concept of only one agency for each major purpose of government. It is sometimes contended that benefits arise out of competition among agencies with overlapping responsibilities. There are also objections raised against "superdepartments" on the grounds of alleged unmanageability or the submersion of important programs.

My response is that many examples can be cited of the destructive consequences of the scattering of related programs among two or more agencies, while I am hard pressed to list one instance in which such fragmentation has proved beneficial to the public interest or was conducive to better management.

With respect to the alleged benefits of competition among agencies, there seems to be some feeling that the resulting struggles over turf will make the contending agencies "try harder" or give citizens a choice in seeking a service. Anyone who examines the long competition between the Corps of Engineers and the Bureau of Reclamation over water resources projects, or that between the old Navy and War Departments over defense resources, or that between the Interior and the Agriculture Departments over the management of public lands, will find that added costs and destructive conflicts have been the primary results. It is possible that a few sophisticated organized groups may learn to advance their interests because of such interagency rivalries, but it is unlikely that the public interest has ever been served by the confusion and duplication that result when closely related programs are placed in different agencies.

Concern over the manageability of large departments has little basis in fact. I have never been able to discern a negative correlation between size and the quality of departmental management. The same applies to independent agencies. Citing the difficulty encountered in managing HEW does not make the case, partly because with all its defects it has done as well as some smaller departments. Moreover, the principal obstacles to improving HEW's effectiveness have been poorly drafted laws establishing new programs, statutory limitations on the Secretary's authority to manage, and an obsolete internal structure.

In recent years the creation of the Department of Housing and Urban Development, the Department of Transportation, the Department of Energy, and the Department of Defense have moved the government toward increased adherence to the principle under discussion. President Nixon's departmental reorganization proposals of 1971 would have constituted important further progress. We still need to consolidate natural resources programs, programs relating to economic affairs, and programs related to human resources within single departments, as was proposed in 1971 and on other occasions. One hopes that these departments will take their place within the structure of the executive branch in the years to come.

4. *The failure to group related programs in major-purpose agencies inevitably produces a shift of power to the policy and managerial offices grouped around the President.* When programmatic interrelationships exist, there must be provision for coordination or undesirable inconsistencies or lapses will occur in carrying out the involved services. Ideally, coordination is accomplished by the head of the agency or department concerned with the major purpose to which the specific programs most closely relate. In those instances in which programs requiring coordination are scattered among separate and often competing departments and agencies, the Executive Office of the President tends to be forced into the process of administration. This has been the case in the field of water resources over a period of many years. The Bureau of the Budget (and subsequently the Office of Management and Budget) has had to play an active role in assuring that what the various agencies concerned with water resources programs undertook to do was consistent with sound river basin development and was based on defensible calculations of costs and benefits.

In the energy area it was necessary to have intense White House involvement in program administration until the establishment of a Department of Energy. James Schlesinger initially served as President Carter's energy adviser, but he quickly concluded that to oversee and coordinate the numerous agencies concerned with energy programs required the creation of an executive department. Schlesinger made a major contribution to the capacity of the federal government to administer and coordinate its energy activities by pursuing successfully, with the support of the President, the establishment of the Department of Energy. It is unfortunate that the legislation creating the department did not adhere to a number of the propositions set forth in this chapter. While the Department of Energy is a great improvement over the fragmentation that preceded its establishment, it has not been able to achieve the leadership role or to administer programs with the effectiveness that might reasonably have been expected of it.

5. *Significant defects in organization cannot be overcome solely by the efforts of a leader or a competent staff and must therefore be addressed directly if effective management is to be achieved.* Among the most frequently heard contentions in the field of government management is the allegation that if good people can be placed in an agency, the organization will make little difference.

This is nonsense. The most important aspect of organizational design is the determination of the mission or scope of authority of an organization. If this is poorly handled, the result can be frustration for the most talented agency head, even if he is supported by a superior and motivated staff. To make this point all we need to do is take the example of the Secretary of the Interior. That department has had some fine secretaries, but none has been able to provide real leadership in the management of the nation's natural resources. There is no way in which the Secretary can bring about the kind of responses from the Corps of Engineers or the Department of Agriculture needed to produce an effective, integrated natural resources strategy or carry it out in practice. Only when programs with close relationships are under the same official is it possible for that official to bring his talents to bear and achieve the results expected of him.

Secretaries of Commerce have for many years striven to achieve a position of leadership in matters of economic policy, but they have rarely succeeded in this objective. Too many of the programs and responsibilities bearing on the nation's economy are now lodged in the Department of the Treasury, the Department of Labor, and independent agencies such as the Small Business Administration and the Federal Reserve System. Secretaries of Commerce are, in fact, usually excluded from the Troika* and other central economic coordination and planning groups.

Similarly if a departmental Secretary's authority over the internal management of his agency has been incumbered by statutory restrictions, he can be prevented from making those changes required to bring about improved management in his department. The efforts of Secretary Weinberger and Undersecretary Carlucci in 1973 and 1974 to decentralize the Department of Health, Education, and Welfare and improve the integration of services delivery in the field were gravely impeded by statutory prohibitions against decentralization and by the placement of authority in subordinate officials of the department. In spite of the skill of these two experienced officials and the assistance of an excellent staff, the reuslts of a two-year effort proved disappointing because they were unable to overcome the numerous limitations on their authority to manage.

6. *All authority over programs and internal management vested in a department or agency of the executive branch should be lodged in the Secretary or administrator with authority to delegate.* It is cutomary for the Congress to place statutory authority over programs in officials of the executive departments and agencies rather than in the President for redelegation. The same is true of many administrative powers. This practice does not of itself cause too much difficulty, for the President has acquired the means to influence or control how agency heads exercise their discretionary powers. Problems do arise, however, when the Congress lodges statutory functions in the heads of bureaus and comparable subdepartmental entities.

The first Hoover Commission, in its *Report on Departmental Management,*[6] described the impediments that this practice could place in the way

---

* The Troika is composed of the Director of the Office of Management and Budget, the Chairman of the Council of Economic Advisers and Secretary of the Treasury.

of the head of a department controlling his agency and making those adjustments required to assure effective management. As a result of the recommendations of the commission, the President transmitted, and the Congress accepted, a number of reorganization plans that removed the authorities of inferior officials and lodged them directly in the Secretaries. The policy of vesting statutory powers only in the agency head was subsequently adhered to in the establishment of the Federal Aviation Agency and the National Aeronautics and Space Administration in 1958 and in the creation of the Environmental Protection Agency in 1970. It was also followed, with a few specific exceptions, for certain recent departments, especially HUD and DOT. While not all agency heads took full advantage of the authority given them by these reforms, they opened the way for strong Secretaries and agency heads to make changes needed to improve the effectiveness of administration within their organizations. Accountability for actions taken was also clarified since the agency head was now fully responsible. There remain instances, including the Department of Health, Education, and Welfare* and the Department of Energy, in which authorities have been placed at levels below the Secretary, and in which the Secretary has been so limited by specific administrative provisions that his latitude over internal structures and systems has been seriously circumscribed. When this is the case, there is inevitably an adverse impact on the quality of internal management. Both the structure and the administrative systems of the department or agency tend to become progressively outdated as changes take place in departmental priorities or in the administrative environment.

It should be emphasized that concentrating statutory powers and presidentially conferred authorities in the head of the agency is quite compatible with the decentralized management discussed subsequently in this chapter. All that is needed is for the Secretary or administrator to have the right to delegate his authorities as he deems desirable. In fact, it is easier to decentralize when the agency head is clearly responsible than when it is necessary to prod lower level officials into delegating powers vested directly in them.

---

\* HEW has since been divested of most of its education functions as the result of legislation creating a Department of Education. HEW is now the Department of Health and Social Services.

*7. More is to be gained by the granting of broad discretion over internal management to the head of an agency than is likely to be lost by the abuse of such authority.* There has been much debate over the authority that a cabinet Secretary or the head of an independent agency should be given over matters of internal management. Involved are the authority to delegate, the authority to establish field offices, the authority to create and abolish internal entities, and a wide range of administrative authorities over such matters as procurement, personnel management, and financial systems.

We have undergone a number of cycles of practice and opinion with respect to the proposition under discussion. As I have previously indicated, the Congress was willing to give NASA and FAA administrators broad grants of authority over the management of their agencies. This policy was also followed in determining the powers to be granted the Secretaries of HUD and DOT when those departments were established. Recently, it has proved more difficult to obtain legislation granting the scope of authority suggested by this proposition and by most theories of management. This reluctance to place adequate authority in the head of an agency appears to be part of a larger development. The Congress, in reaction to the problems of recent administrations, is now inclined to place more checks on the freedom of the President and other officials of the executive branch to exercise discretion in the administration of the laws. The many detailed provisions governing internal structure and the authority of the Secretary set forth in the recent Department of Energy legislation is a case in point. One need only contrast that department's organic statute with the 1966 legislation establishing a Department of Transportation to note the wide differences in the approach taken to secretarial authority. Unfortunately, the more the discretion of the President and the heads of agencies is confined in the interest of preventing abuses, the more their capacity to manage well is curtailed. Our system provides better ways of identifying and correcting abuses than rigid statutory provisions that prevent a Secretary from administering his department.

The recent legislation creating statutory Inspectors General in most departments is inconsistent with the proposition under discussion. In theory the Inspector General position will help assure that an agency administers its programs with integrity and that audit and investigative functions are vigorously pursued under a high level official. In reality the creation of a statutory Inspector General interferes with the authority of the Secretary to arrange internally for the investigative and audit functions to be performed in the manner best suited to the needs of his department. The existence of an Inspector General further weakens and fragments the authority of the once important post of Assistant Secretary for Administration.

In the past, the responsibility for audit and for the investigation of allegations of corruption were important adjuncts to the other managerial functions performed by a number of Assistant Secretaries for Administration on behalf of the Secretary. In its original concept the Assistant Secretary for Administration was a career official with a sophisticated knowledge of the department. He was therefore able to assure a continuity and vigor of audit and investigative functions not easily achievable under the leadership of short-term political appointees. It is, of course, appropriate to require each Secretary to establish machinery compatible with the management systems of his department to carry out the functions now being entrusted by law to the Inspector Generals, just as heads of agencies are expected to place the responsibility for management improvement in some designated official. It is not necessary to achieve effective internal audit and to prevent corruption to impose on a Secretary a presidential appointee over whom he has little control.

8. *While there is no such thing as a preferred span of control generally applicable to federal agencies, a narrow span of control should normally be avoided since it submerges functions of direct concern to the head of the agency.* I agree with those writers who have challenged the rigid span of control theory articulated by early students of management and organization. Each agency has an institutional setting and a range of functions that influence the span of control best suited to its management. Furthermore, span of control is one aspect of organizational design that should take into account the management style of the head of the organization and the quality of the staff available to him.

In designing an organization, note should be taken of the effect of a narrow span on the access of important staff to the head of the agency. The fewer the officials that are allowed direct access to the Secretary or agency head, the narrower the organizational pyramid will become. This means that officials whose functions may be of substantial significance and sensitivity from the standpoint of the head of the agency may be placed far down in the organization. When the formal organization charts of a department, or any subdivision thereof, set forth a narrow span of control, there is a tendency to bypass the channels indicated on the official charts. The realities of departmental administration tend to force the Secretary and Deputy Secretary to deal directly with a larger number of their subordinates than may be contemplated by the formal organization.

What this proposition says is that the span of control of an executive department or agency should be determined by the number of programs whose importance warrant direct access to the top leadership of the agency. This approach is a pragmatic one that will normally result in a minimum of four to as many as seven or eight major program officials reporting to the Secretary or agency head. A Secretary equipped with a competent deputy will normally encounter little difficulty in supervising and coordinating a span within this range; in addition, he can maintain direct relationships with the heads of a number of staff offices.

Special care should ordinarily be taken to avoid dividing the operating programs of an agency between two deputies to the Secretary or administrator. Any such arrangement not only entails the disadvantages associated with an extremely narrow span of control, but can also threaten the stability of the organization. In 1950, supervision of the Commerce Department's line programs was divided between an Undersecretary for Transportation and the Undersecretary of the department. The Undersecretaries for Transportation quickly came to see themselves as officials at war with the rest of the department, and they regarded the departmental staff around the Secretary and Undersecretary as unsympathetic to the transportation mission. As a result, most Undersecretaries of Commerce for Transportation actively encouraged the formation of a separate Department of Transportation. It is noteworthy that the last Undersecretary for Transportation, Alan Boyd, became the first DOT Secretary.

When the Office of Management and Budget superseded the Bureau of the Budget in 1970, the management functions and budget functions were grouped respectively under two major officials reporting to the director. From the beginning of this arrangement there were tensions between the "M" and Budget "sides" of the OMB. These tensions were much sharper than those which existed in the old Bureau of Budget, where the major functions of the bureau were divided among a half dozen equivalents of assistant directors.

9. *In designing the internal structure of a department or agency, care should be taken to avoid placing a disproportionate share of the manpower and resources in a single operating entity.* Experience suggests that any program element of a department or agency that becomes extraordinarily strong from a standpoint of size, scope of functions, or the financial resources available to it in relation to other program entities will complicate the management problems of the agency head and his staff offices. Such dominant organizations expect to influence the policies and administrative practices of the department to a degree greater than the other program entities, and they are often successful in doing so. The great size of the dominant program element and the stronger staff it can assemble on behalf of its aspirations will in fact normally lead to a domination of the department. This phenomenon tends to produce continuing friction and tension within the agency. Should the major program element conclude that it cannot win acceptance of the positions it advocates, it strives for increased autonomy or even separate status. I have already cited what happened to the Department of Commerce when much of the department's total staff and resources came to be lodged under an Undersecretary for Transportation. Years ago, the strength of the Bureau of Reclamation in the Department of the Interior created problems for the central management. The FBI in the Department of Justice and at times the Social Security Administration in the Department of Health, Education, and Welfare have also presented special problems because of their large size and influence within their respective departments.

Most recently, I have observed the adverse impact on the U.S. Railway Association, a government corporation, of the growth in the magnitude of its legal functions. As the General Counsel came to acquire one-half the staff and nearly two-thirds of the administrative budget, it became increasingly difficult for the Board of Directors and the President of USRA to exercise control over the legal programs. The General Counsel's drive for increased self-sufficiency and for the authority to escape controls applicable to other offices also complicated the job of staff officials administering USRA-wide systems.

10. *Every effort should be made to group internal administrative management functions in a single staff official reporting directly to the head of*

*an agency.* The Secretary of an executive department or the administrator of an independent agency needs to be able to rely upon a knowledgeable official to assist him in assuring that the internal administration of the department or agency is in good order, especially with respect to the so-called administrative management functions. This proposition warrants consideration because of the intimate interrelationships that exist between the various functions that contribute in a staff or support capacity to the effective execution of an agency's programs. Included are personnel administration, financial management, management systems development, management information, support services, and procurement and contracting. If one official is in a position to oversee and coordinate these vital activities, the agency head can be freed to concentrate on the substantive policy and external relationship matters to which he should be giving his primary attention.

In the Federal Aviation Agency, the Department of Transportation, the U.S. Railway Association, and a number of other departments, agencies, and government corporations, the existence of a comprehensive administrative management official produced results that were clearly beneficial to the agency head. In agencies in which there was a failure to provide promptly for a center of administrative management leadership, serious delays resulted in establishing the agency and in developing the systems of management required for its effective functioning. Examples are AMTRAK, the Department of Energy, and the National Consumer Cooperative Bank.

There has been a tendency to separate so-called controller or financial functions from such general administrative responsibilities as personnel management, support services, management systems design, and the overseeing of procurement. This has usually proved to be undesirable. Such a division was tried in the Department of Health, Education, and Welfare for a number of years and significantly weakened administrative management leadership within the department. Eventually, all administrative functions except personnel management were consolidated under a single Assistant Secretary and the position of Controller was abolished.

The Department of Energy suffers from a unusual degree of fragmentation of administrative management leadership. The department contains a Director of Administration, a Controller, and still another official responsible for procurement and contracting. The creation of the post of Inspector General has produced additional fragmentation. Thus, while Secretary Boyd or Secretary Volpe in the early days of the Department of

Transportation could look to one person for assistance in virtually all aspects of internal management, the Secretary of Energy is not in this fortunate position.

Budget functions deserve special attention. It has long been a point of controversy whether the administration of a departmental budget should be placed under the Assistant Secretary for Administration or be lodged under some other official. I am inclined to regard budget as more a substantive program review activity than an internal administrative management function. For this reason, the placement of budget outside the Assistant Secretary for Administration can be undertaken in some departmental settings without a serious departure from the proposition under discussion. On the other hand, it often develops, especially in smaller agencies, that the official charged with other administrative management functions is the best equipped to assure that the budget administration proceeds smoothly. It should be noted here that budget and accounting are different functions. Therefore, if the budget is placed under an official charged with program review and resource allocation (as is now the case in the Department of Transportation), such operations as financial reporting, accounting, and payroll should remain with the principal administrative management officer.

Special attention must be given to the background and qualifications of the person charged with the oversight of administrative management activities. Agency management in the executive branch is a specialized occupation, and substantial experience in the administration of internal systems is necessary if an incumbent is to be effective in the position. Recognition of this fact led the first Hoover Commission to recommend the creation of the post of Assistant Secretary for Administration and to urge that it be in career service.[7] The fact that an agency may choose to place its senior administrative management officer outside the competitive civil service no way reduces the importance of seeking an incumbent who is experienced in getting things done within a federal agency and who knows how to render sophisticated advice to the political leadership in the use of available internal management tools.

11. *Decentralization of decision-making authority to operating levels close to those being served has so often proved advantageous that the retention of authority in the central offices of federal agencies should be required*

*to bear the burden of proof.* Most departments and major independent agencies perform the services for which they were created through field staffs, since those services are provided to individual citizens or to state and local governments located throughout the United States.

The design of a field organization includes the establishment of regional and subregional offices and the distribution of employees in the field. It also involves crucial decisions concerning the amount of authority to be vested in the field officials. To the extent that the field staff is authorized to take final action on matters falling within the program authority of the agency, the organization is considered decentralized. If the field staff must refer matters coming before them to the headquarters for review or approval prior to definitive action, the agency is regarded as functioning in a centralized mode.

Most new agencies begin as centralized entities. This is because the headquarters is usually established before the field offices can be created and also because it is difficult to decentralize until an agency has established basic policies and priorities and until it has been able to equip its field officials with the knowledge which they need to exercise delegated authority. Ideally, an agency moves authority to field officials as the conditions for effective decentralization are met. Unfortunately, headquarters staff are often resistant to placing authority in field personnel. Persuasive reasons are put forth by headquarters staff in support of their retaining various approval authorities, even after the field organization is fully prepared to receive additional delegations.

The retention in headquarters of the responsibility for approving individual actions when a competent field organization is in place tends to delay the processing of matters before the agency and wastes manpower in duplicative reviews. It also frustrates the work of Federal Regional Councils and other mechanisms for bringing about coordinated field action by two or more agencies. Headquarters staffs in mature organizations function best when they are concerned with questions of policy, program development, priorities in the allocation of resources, audit and evaluation, and the rendering of assistance in specialized matters for which the regions cannot be equipped. To the extent that central staff is diverted to redoing the work of field officials, functions that can be performed only in the headquarters will tend to be neglected.

The experience gained in decentralization in the Federal Aviation Agency, the Department of Transportation, the Department of Defense, the Department of HEW, and the Department of HUD suggests strongly that more efficient, more timely, and more sensitive management results from the shifting of *operating* authorities to the field. In determining the optimum degree of decentralization for an agency it is desirable to insist that headquarters officials who urge the retention of authority to approve individual actions initiated in the field carry the burden of proof. In determining the validity of the arguments presented by headquarters officials on behalf of withholding authority regional personnel should be consulted and be given an opportunity to make their case.

12. *Comprehensive regional directors should be established only in agencies in which the substantive field operations involve programs requiring significant coordination at the service delivery level.* Another crucial aspect of design of a field organization involves the desirability of establishing regional directors to coordinate those programs and functions carried out by the department or agency on a decentralized basis. Some studies, such as that of the Ash Council, have urged the creation of departmental regional directors in settings in which they would serve little useful purpose and might actually impede field administration. This proposition holds that a departmental regional director will be a constructive factor in field management only when there is a need for such an official to assure that related field operations are consistently administered in a coordinated manner. If the programs of a department require little in the way of field coordination, as is the case in the Department of Treasury and the Justice Department, no need exists for a comprehensive regional director. Such departments properly rely on each program entity to establish such field offices and regions as it may require.

Departments like Transportation, Agriculture, and Labor have programs with some field interfaces, yet the degree of coordination required does not warrant the insertion of departmental regional directors in the command channels between the program elements and their field staffs. These departments tend to rely on weak regional directors or secretarial representatives who carry out a number of facilitative, informational, and representational functions but who do not have the authority to direct operations within the regions. Unified agencies in which the operating programs have significant field interfaces, such as the Department of Housing and Urban Development and the Environmental Protection Agency, usually rely on comprehensive regional directors to bring about needed coordination in the regions. This approach is to be preferred to requiring all matters involving overlap or conflict to be resolved in the headquarters.

In 1961, the Federal Aviation Agency, then an independent agency, established strong regional directors because it determined, after two years of operation, that its various aviation programs required close oversight and coordination by an official nearer the scene than the Washington headquarters. The FAA then moved from a highly centralized administration to strong regional directors with broad decentralized authority over program matters. The results proved beneficial to the management of the FAA, and several thousand positions were eliminated in the next four years in the face of an increasing workload.

13. *No head of an agency should be expected to direct or coordinate the work of his peers as a substitute for coming to grips with deficiencies in executive branch organization.* Frequently efforts are made to compensate for the dispersion of responsibility for related programs among several agencies through the establishment of a committee or council chaired by the head of one of the agencies concerned. Alternatively, an agency head may be charged with a "leadership" role in bringing about concerted action on the part of other officials.

If there is any proposition that appears to have general application, it is that arrangements of this kind prove disappointing when measured by results. President Nixon attempted in 1973 to establish a group of counselors for domestic programs and to require that the heads of other departments and agencies with related responsibilities report to the President through those counselors. This experiment was unsuccessful, and it was quietly abandoned during the Watergate investigations.

The water resources area has been replete with coordinating committees. During the period immediately after World War II the Federal Interagency River Basin Committee and its successor, the Interagency Committee on Water Resources, tried under the chairmanship of the Secretary of the Interior to play a coordinating role in river basin planning and water resources project development. These coordinating committees proved unsuccessful in coming to grips with the basic need for unified administration of the nation's water resources.

In the period prior to the establishment of the FAA an elaborate mechanism called the Air Coordinating Committee sought to foster coordination in aviation matters under the chairmanship of the Undersecretary of Commerce for Transportation. Its inability to come to grips with the nation's major aviation problems was an important factor in the creation of the FAA. Once the FAA was in place the ACC disappeared from the scene.*

Usually, the assignment of the Secretary of a department or the head of an agency to a coordinating committee chairmanship or leadership role is undertaken to avoid the more painful need to come to grips with fundamental defects in executive branch organization. Usually the defenders of the status quo contend that all that is needed is "policy" coordination and that it will then be easy for the separate departments and agencies to administer their respective programs in a consistent manner. This happy outcome almost never takes place, and government administration suffers from a continuation of the fragmented execution of related activities. The solution, as suggested by the FAA-ACC example, is usually a reorganization that equips a single official with the authority to bring about effective coordination.

14. *The existing organization of an executive department or agency should not be tampered with unless the reasons for making changes are fully understood and a plan to deal with identified problems has been developed.* No matter how defective an organization may seem to be on paper, it learns to function to some degree and adapt itself to certain of the realities of its administrative environment. For this reason, it is undesirable to disturb an organization simply because external criticism or an examination of charts raises questions concerning the soundness of the structure.

New officials, including newly inaugurated Presidents, should take care to assure that the weaknesses of existing structures have been documented

---

* The Air Coordinating Committee was established by Executive Order 9781, 19 September 1946. It was terminated by Executive Order 10883, 11 August 1960, and its functions were transferred to the Federal Aviation Agency.

and that workable solutions have been devised before undertaking to reorganize. It is important to resist the impulse to regard what was inherited from a predecessor administration or official as necessarily defective and in need of change. It is also advisable to reject the psychological compulsion to reorganize simply to make one's mark on an inherited organization. All reorganizations entail costs, and there is a need to be sure that contemplated changes, however attractive superficially, will produce real benefits.

Some of the most serious mistakes in the design of executive agencies have arisen out of commitments made without the President or other involved administration officials having sufficient information as to need or alternative solutions. A recent example is the decision to proceed with the breaking up of the Department of Health, Education, and Welfare and the creation of a new Department of Education without adequate consideration of the alternative of creating a unified and modern Department of Human Resources. The decision of the Secretary of HEW in 1977 to abolish the regional directors, which undid years of work in strengthening the field organization of that department, is another instance of a course of action being launched without a full understanding of the need or the consequences.

If Presidents, staff officials of the Executive Office of the President, heads of departments and agencies, and members of Congress could be encouraged to take a systems approach to the identification of organizational weaknesses in the executive branch and in the design of measures to correct such deficiencies as are found to exist, more progress would be made in improving federal management.

15. *When an improvement in executive branch organization is needed and a solution can be developed, persistence when combined with a sense of tactics can often overcome even the strongest resistance.* We deal with a system in which the President, the Congress, the personalities of agency officials, and the views of organized groups can all affect the feasibility of bringing about improvements in organizational design. It is therefore necessary that we consider the techniques that have been used successfully in overcoming obstacles to administrative reforms.

There have been agencies of the executive branch, such as the Reconstruction Finance Corporation, the Atomic Energy Commission, and the independent U.S. Maritime Commission, which once appeared to be permanent institutions in spite of the fact that alternative approaches to the organization of their functions seemed to be desirable. In each instance, initial plans to abolish the agency and transfer its functions to a more appropriate departmental setting had to be deferred because the opposition could not be overcome.

None of these three agencies now exists. In the case of the Reconstruction Finance Corporation, well-publicized scandals eased the task of the President and Bureau of the Budget in winning acceptance for proposals to liquidate the agency. The U.S. Maritime Commission was similarly done in by a scandal that made it difficult for the Congress to reject plans to place the maritime functions under the Secretary of Commerce. In the case of the Atomic Energy Commission, growing energy concerns led first to its replacement by an independent Energy Research and Development Administration. Shortly thereafter, ERDA was placed in the Department of Energy where its research programs could make a direct contribution to the mission of the new department. These historical examples illustrate that it is first necessary to identify weaknesses in the structure of the executive branch and design appropriate plans for bringing about desired changes in organization. It is then desirable to win the acquiescence of those officials, members of Congress, and citizen groups whose support or neutrality is essential to bring about a proposed reform. If it proves initially difficult to overcome opposition to a reorganization, those concerned with bringing about the needed changes should take a long view of the situation and be prepared to exploit any development that might have the effect of increasing support or weakening opposition.

An example of where patience eventually was rewarded is the creation of the Department of Transportation. Staff of the Bureau of the Budget had favored the establishment of the Department of Transportation in the late 1940s, but the Hoover Commission preferred instead to recommend a consolidated Department of Commerce and Transportation. Several years later, Bureau of the Budget staff again raised the desirability of establishing a Department of Transportation when it became apparent that aviation functions would be removed from the Department of Commerce and given independent status. Once more bureau staff were frustrated, this time by the opposition of Secretary of Commerce Sinclair Weeks. Only a few years later, however, the support of FAA Administrator Najeeb Halaby opened the way for President Johnson to recommend a Department of Transportation. This time the proposal became law within a matter of months. The same patience may eventually produce a Department of Natural Resources and a more effective arrangement for the administration of the nation's economic programs.

The fifteen propositions discussed in this paper are by no means a comprehensive list of the lessons learned over the years in the design of government structures. The list does, however, include those major propositions that seem to deserve the most careful consideration by any official or adviser concerned with the role, structure, or management of an agency of the executive branch. Since the conditions encountered in addressing each organizational need will vary, there must be an awareness that what may be the solution in one situation may have to be modified in another. Nevertheless, if the designer of an organization will assure himself that what he seeks to do is either compatible with the above propositions or departs from them for clearly identified and persuasive reasons, his efforts are likely to be accompanied by success. At a minimum, he will avoid most of the errors that persons lacking practical experience in the establishment of federal executive agencies so often make.

## NOTES

1. See Luther Gulick and L. Urwick, ed., *Papers on the Science of Administration* (New York: Institute of Public Administration, 1937).
2. University of Alabama Press, 1967.
3. 2nd ed.; New York: Oxford University Press, 1977.
4. See President's Committee on Administrative Management, *Report with Special Studies* (Washington, D.C.: Government Printing Office, 1937).
5. See *Papers Relating to the President's Departmental Reorganization Program* (Washington, D.C.: Government Printing Office, 1972).
6. *Commission on Organization of the Executive Branch of the Government* ("Report on Departmental Management"), 1949.
7. Ibid.

# 8

# Implementing Reorganization*

## I. M. DESTLER

For reorganization, as for any other change, implementation is the bottom line. Without it, the whole exercise is show and symbolism. Yet in real-life attempts at reorganization, serious concern with implementation is typically too little and too late. Enormous attention is devoted to analyzing and deciding what changes should be made. The problem of getting from here to there is addressed only belatedly. To paraphrase Erwin Hargrove, implementation often seems the "missing link" in reorganization.[1] One purpose of this chapter is to explore why.

There are two broad ways of defining implementation. The first centers on the concrete steps required to make formal reorganization decisions effective and complete—drafting orders, getting needed legislative action, reallocating money and personnel slots, bringing on new staff, juggling office space. The second, more ambitious definition is linked to purpose; implementation here is tied to actual behavioral change, achieving the alterations in governmental process or outcome (e.g., efficiency, shifted priorities, improved coordination) that were the reorganization's goal. Focus on the latter leads to consideration of broader issues, overlapping those treated in most of the other chapters.

Following this general distinction, this chapter begins by reviewing the major steps required to make reorganization formally effective. It then

* This chapter draws on several helpful conversations with present and former officials responsible for implementing particular reorganizations.

moves to the more interesting question of what affects whether support for implementation can be mobilized and maintained. In so doing, it addresses some of the ways that neglect of implementation seems built into the reorganization process.

Because the basic premise is that the executive is sponsoring reorganization, I will mention only in passing one recurrent implementation problem —that which arises when a reorganization program is built around a central recommendation the executive does not endorse. For example, the Herter Committee on Foreign Affairs Personnel gave careful attention to implementation in *Personnel for the New Diplomacy* (December 1962), but based its strategy on a proposal that Secretary of State Dean Rusk opposed and effectively tabled: appointment of a new "number three" state official, an Executive Undersecretary. With its central vehicle thus sidetracked, the implementation of other Herter recommendations was, not surprisingly, limited.

## Concrete Problems

Implementation can be analyzed most directly in terms of the specific things that must be done to translate a general reorganization decision into an operating reality. Stephen K. Bailey wrote in 1968 that "the *essential* controls of an agency head over constituent units are three, and only three: (1) control of legislative proposals; (2) control of budgetary totals; (3) control of major personnel appointments and assignments."[2] Not surprisingly, these correspond closely to the major resources involved in implementing reorganization—with one addition, the allocation of office space.

### Laws and Regulations

Once an executive opts for a particular reorganization, he must assure that his decision has the required legal standing. This will always require drafting and issuance of internal orders within the agency affected. It will often require an executive order or equivalent presidential action document.* It

* National Security reorganizations have typically employed orders from a separate classified series: NSAMs (National Security Action Memoranda), NSDMs (National Security Decision Memoranda), and currently PDs (Presidential Directives).

will sometimes require changes in statute, achievable either through reorganization plan (if the Congress has extended this authority to the President, as it did for Carter in 1977-80) or through the normal legislative process. Use of the latter is required, under current law, if the proposal involves creation of a new executive department, abolishing an executive department or independent regulatory agency, or establishing or continuing agencies or functions beyond what current law authorizes.

In cases where the executive has some choice among these instruments, or in his relative reliance on them, the tradeoff is fairly straightforward. Changing a statute has the greatest visibility and credibility, and conveys the broadest legitimacy on reorganization. It also contributes to permanence. But it most restricts executive flexibility, inviting Congress to specify the details of administration. Internal memoranda have the opposite advantages and drawbacks. And the recent trend in statutes has been toward increased congressional specificity, making the Department of Energy, created in 1977, harder to administer than the Department of Transportation established ten and one-half years before.

Public administration doctrine has long favored the more flexible instruments and less specificity in statutes in order to give Presidents and cabinet members greater leeway in running and restructuring their own domains. Thus Bureau of Budget/OMB has periodically sought to replace statutory with Executive Order authorities, as when, in the Johnson administration, a reorganization plan abolished the National Advisory Committee on Financial and Monetary Problems (NAC), and the President simultaneously created by Executive Order the National Advisory Committee on Monetary and Financial *Policies* (NAC). Separate statutory existence, however, facilitates separate congressional funding for an agency or function, even if its prime role is to advise the President. This was apparently one reason, for example, why the Nixon administration sought a statutory base for the Council on International Economic Policy, originally created by presidential memorandum in 1971. Congress provided this in August 1972.

For those seeking to carry out a particular organizational mandate, a statute or executive order is often important to their credibility. President Ford's Economic Policy Board, the most effective broad policy coordinating vehicle in his administration, was based on Executive Order 11808, issued

30 September 1974, less than two months after he took office. Carter abolished the board through Executive Order 11975, then used a simple memorandum to give a similarly broad coordinating mandate to his Economic Policy *Group.* Those in the EOP and Treasury seeking to buttress the group's standing as the prime presidential economic policy review channel worked, in the spring of 1977, to get a formal executive order for the EPG. But Carter's Executive Office reorganization staff, at work in this same period, saw such an order as preempting its recommendations and persuaded the Secretary of the Treasury to accept its deferral until completion of the overall EOP study. The study in fact led to changes that made the group much less formal, and much less a regular decision channel to the President. The draft Executive Order was never resurrected.

In cases where particular sensitivity to Congress is required for an agency's functioning, statutory entrenchment may be a blessing. Costs in executive flexibility may be more than offset by the stabilizing effect on management of a potentially volatile issue. The role of the Office of the Special Representative for Trade Negotiations, for example, was strengthened by the fact that it was created—and later reinforced—at congressional initiative. In particular, this buttressed STR's relationship with the key trade committees, Senate Finance and House Ways and Means.

For any new agency performing functions specified in statute, one crucial implementation step is assuring that it has, on its first day of operation, all the legal authority for these functions and that the necessary internal orders exist for assigning these functions within the agency. The major functions of the Department of Housing and Urban Development, created by statute in 1965, were those of the Housing and Home Finance Agency. The legislation specified that HUD would come into existence sixty days after the President signed the statute, with its Secretary assuming all the functions of HHFA. But when the date arrived, President Johnson had appointed no Secretary! The result was that HHFA Administrator Robert Weaver (who later did become Secretary) had to try to keep the programs going without a firm legal basis for doing so. The next department created by the Johnson administration, Transportation, avoided such a problem through provisions in its statute that it would come into being ninety days *after* its Secretary took office or at an earlier date if the President so specified. Subsequent statutes have generally followed this formula.

## Budgeting

When an agency, new or old, assumes a function previously performed elsewhere, it must get control of the funds necessary to do so. To this end, statutes typically authorize transfer of such "unexpended balances of appropriations, allocations and other funds employed" as the OMB director determines are linked to these functions. If the amounts involved do not follow automatically from the functions, such determinations are generally preceded by an adversary process, between the gaining and losing agency, brokered by the responsible OMB staff officer.

Budgetary changes can also help implement reorganization in other ways. If the goal is to reinforce an existing cabinet secretary vis-à-vis subordinate units, a budget planning process that sharpens tradeoffs at his level is a vital means. So it can be also, at least potentially, for a Secretary of State with an interdepartmental leadership mandate—hence proposals for a comprehensive foreign affairs budget or programming system. Conversely, if the aim is to give a subunit greater autonomy—as the Carter administration in 1979 provided the Peace Corps within ACTION, for example—budgetary tradeoffs and budget staffing need to be decentralized, to reinforce the subunit head.

A different sort of shift is required if the reorganization decision is to change the primary internal division of labor—making regions rather than functions the prime subdivision, for example. When this step was undertaken at AID, it meant that budgetary allocations had to be primarily among countries and regions, and tradeoffs among food production, health, heavy industry development, and so forth, should be treated, to the extent possible, within each country program rather than at the level of the administrator.

Implementation of a reorganization may also require changes in how OMB reviews an agency budget. Autonomy is advanced, for example, by giving a subunit a separate OMB ceiling for budget planning purposes.

## Personnel

Perhaps most important, reorganizations are implemented through decisions about people—where they work, what they do. The most general personnel decisions, of course, involve establishing ranks and titles of officials created by the reorganization, providing personnel ceilings for new organizations, and adjusting them for old ones. Here also, "determination orders" by the OMB director are the established means of allocating and transferring positions. The numbers are often bitterly contested. When the Carter trade reorganization plan of 1979 transferred responsibility for U.S. commercial attaches overseas from State to Commerce, Secretary of State Cyrus Vance went personally to OMB Director James McIntyre to protest the proposed transfer of about thirty-five related Washington positions and won about five of them back. Agencies will also seek maximum flexibility in using the positions they gain or retain—to limit, for example, the number of unwanted incumbents they must take along with the job slots.

Probably the most crucial implementing action involving personnel is the timely placement of persons committed to a reorganization in key leadership positions. Johnson's Department of Transportation profited from the early appointment of Alan Boyd as Secretary, and the prior general expectation that he would get the job. Similarly, the primary reason why Carter's Peace Corps autonomy decision had some prospect of being implemented was that the newly designated Peace Corps director, Richard Celeste, helped to shape it and saw it as crucial to his Washington success. By contrast, Carter's Federal Emergency Management Agency (FEMA) suffered because of the tardy designation of its director. Or officials may be in place but uninterested. In March 1966, for example, President Johnson issued National Security Action Memorandum 341 creating a new network of interagency committees to coordinate foreign policy; the ranking committee, the Senior Interdepartmental Group (SIG), was to be headed by the Undersecretary of State. But the occupant of that post, George Ball, was uninterested in the reform and preparing to leave government anyway. His successor, Nicholas Katzenbach, took an interest only well after his appointment when President Johnson, apparently at staff initiative, asked him when he was going to hold a meeting of the SIG.

The prospect that a well-regarded individual will head a new organization can contribute to favorable congressional action—as with Thomas Ehrlich and the International Development Cooperation Agency. Conversely, Congress may balk if members have reservations. The Federal Security Administration (later HEW) was not made a department under Truman, and one factor was concern that Federal Security Administrator Oscar Ewing would be named Secretary if it was.

Having the right people in the right positions has also been crucial for foreign service personnel reform. In the Macomber program of 1970-72, the official directly responsible for implementing most of the approved changes was the Director General of the Foreign Service, who reported directly to Macomber. But neither of the two men who held this post during this period was particularly sympathetic to the reform program or committed to its implementation. The Wriston program inaugurated in 1954 was a striking contrast; even before the public report was issued, Wriston Committee member Charles Saltzman was moving into the special post of Undersecretary for Administration created to implement the reforms, and although he held this job for only seven months, he was succeeded by Deputy Undersecretary Loy Henderson, also committed to Wristonization, who stayed on for six years.

More generally, practitioners of reorganization generally agree that the post most important to fill early, aside from that of head of a new agency, is that of chief administrative official. If this person is not in place to orchestrate slots, money, space, and management procedures when the major program subordinates are designed, they are likely to make separate uncoordinated decisions, which must be modified later, or to reach for control of particular matters in order to secure their own turf. For as one veteran implementer puts it, reorganization "sets loose strivings in people." It also sets loose fears that if they don't grab what is theirs today, it won't be there tomorrow. A strong, fair central administrator cannot eliminate such strivings, but he can arbitrate among the strivers and bring some order to their operating environment.

Even when a strongly motivated official is in charge, with a clear mandate, making the required internal personnel changes can be a time-consuming and painful process. Implementation of the decision to give the Peace Corps autonomy within ACTION led, perhaps inevitably, to protracted wrangling over the disposition of particular offices and slots. For ACTION had previously operated as a highly centralized agency, with about two-thirds of its Washington personnel in agency-wide units (e.g., recruitment, medical services, administration support, budget and planning), and only one-third attached to the Peace Corps and the domestic volunteer programs. The Peace Corps director had a strong new executive order, a separate budget and considerable congressional support, but to make his autonomy mandate a reality he and his staff had to fight, function by function, to get slots shifted to his direct control.

## Space

Parkinson has written that the most successful organizations "flourish in shabby and makeshift surroundings," whereas a "perfection of planned layout is achieved only by institutions on the point of collapse." There is some truth here—what makes any organization effective, most of all, is the combination of an important job to perform and the leverage to perform it. Nevertheless, it seems wrong to conclude that the immediate physical environment is unrelated to, or even inversely correlated with, a reorganization's chance of success.

Office space is not always addressed in organizational analyses, but it has both operational and symbolic importance. After the late philosopher Charles Frankel was appointed Assistant Secretary of State for Educational and Cultural Affairs, he was surprised to find himself devoting substantial time to keeping his bureau from being moved out of the main State Department building. But he felt, quite reasonably, that his mandate to raise the visibility and priority of international cultural activities could not remain credible to his staff if they were shifted to less desirable quarters. And within particular buildings, location is often regarded, not inaccurately, as an indication of power. Offices on the seventh floor of the State Department, on the E wing of the Pentagon, and in the Old Executive Office Building speak for themselves. One obvious way to reinforce the officials upon whom a reorganization depends, therefore, is to give them office locations that will be read as signs of presidential or secretarial favor.

Another symbolic way that space can be used to strengthen reorganization is to give a new or restructured agency an attractive central building of its own as soon as possible after its creation. The Department of Energy suffered from the lag between its formal creation and its movement into a central new headquarters. For delay tends to reinforce the impression that nothing has really changed, that the old ways of doing business are going to continue.

And more than appearances are at stake, for location does, in fact, have a direct impact on how officials carry out their day-to-day work. "Nothing 'propinques' like propinquity," and even in the telephone age, the best way to build allegiance to new organizational units and their purposes is to bring people together physically, building up informal as well as formal contact. Conversely, if an aim of reorganization is to break up old working units, then physical separation is an important means to this end. And last but not least, consolidating the space of those in an organization likely to be dealing most regularly with one another brings obvious gains in efficiency—reducing, for example, the time required for sheer physical movement of people and intragovernmental mail.

Why then is space often the last thing to be secured? The answer is that obtaining it can be excruciatingly difficult. The General Services Administration has authority over most federal office space, some of which is owned, some leased. But this is already occupied by agencies determined to keep it or trade it for better. Leasing more existing privately owned space is difficult (at this writing, for example, less than 1 percent of the office space in Washington, D.C., is vacant) and the empty rooms are scattered. New buildings can be built—and are built—but for the government to do so directly takes about seven years, and for it to get a structure built privately for government leasing takes about four years.

Thus the only way to get a central headquarters for a new agency that joins formerly scattered units, or contiguous space for newly consolidated functions, is to dislodge the current occupants. This is never easy. If critics were depressed by how slowly the Department of Energy got a central headquarters, insiders were impressed with how fast—a department was created and moved into one million square feet of centrally located space, the Forrestal Building, within the same presidential term! But it took a presidential order, followed by persistent bureaucratic warfare, to achieve it.

## Putting It All Together

In practice, action on law and regulations, budget, personnel, and space must proceed simultaneously. This typically involves three central federal agencies—the Office of Management and Budget, the General Services Administration, and the Office of Personnel Management—working together and with the specific agencies affected. Ideally, each of the three should maintain a substantial standing competence for implementing reorganization. In practice, this is hard to do because the workload is discontinuous

—there are occasional major reorganizations, like energy, interspersed with many smaller ones, like trade. Thus, in practice, available central staff capacity (and experience with past reorganizations) is often less than needed when a major implementation effort is required.

There is also the prior or simultaneous need to maintain communication with the Congress, particularly the government operations committees, to assure that statutes are enacted in a form consistent with reorganization's purpose, and that there is a receptive voice when experience indicates that amendments are required.

## Implementation as Behavioral Change

Thus far, this chapter has focused mainly on mechanics. But if reorganization is to be real, it must ultimately change the way people do public business. This means that the primary actors in the policy area affected— the bureaucrats, the client groups, and the congressional constituents— must shift to enduring new patterns of behavior. To all these groups, an effective implementation effort must therefore send a twofold signal: that what is happening is real change, with considerable force behind it; and that they can, in most cases, find ways to live with it, even benefit from it, if they cooperate. Without the first message, no one will have reason to depart from business as usual. Without the second, those affected may see resistance as their only option, whatever its risks. Eliciting such behavioral change is particularly complicated, of course, if the target is discretionary behavior of many officials dispersed through the organization.

Looked at this way, implementation becomes not a mechanical process of selecting the appropriate formal devices but a political/behavioral challenge. The starting point is recognition that, at least for large organizations and major programs, no executive can amass the political force necessary to impose enduring change; the resources available for resistance, and the sheer inertia, will simply be too great. But neither clienteles nor career bureaucracies are ever monolithic. Within them are interests that can serve the executive's purpose if he learns how to work with them, reinforce them, and influence them. And they have experience and skills he badly needs— above all, knowledge of existing systems and how to make them work.

Thus conceived, real organizational change is a gradual process, just like any other serious policy enterprise, with the executive using his leverage to elicit not just compliance but support, systematically working with and rewarding those inside and outside groups whose puposes coincide with his own or can be brought to do so. Hugh Heclo and Arnold Kanter are among those whose writings suggest means of achieving this end—working for "conditionally cooperative behavior" rather than absolute loyalty; avoiding frontal challenges to the professional self-esteem of the dominant professional group—such as the McNamara regime mounted, intentionally or not, to the uniformed services. One can also look at promotion systems and ways of influencing what and who they reward. And one can cultivate external constituencies, seeking ways that their interests and needs can be reconciled with a new order. The prerequisite for doing these things is a willingness to grasp the organization in its own terms, to learn what moves bureaucrats within it and the external interests that press in on it, not in order to accept these things as they are but to explore the potential and limits of possible change.

## Why Implementation Is Neglected

Treated as behavioral change, implementation is obviously difficult, and the reasons for its neglect become clearer. As long as reorganization staffs stick to designing proposals for change and maneuvering to get them to executives for decision, their job may not be easy, but at least they are working their own terrain. And as long as the executive sticks to decision making, he is staying on his. But when they move into the details of agency orders, budget processes, personnel allocations, even office space allocation, they enter an alien domain. They move from a process with one central decider —the executive—or one focused decision process—enactment of a law by Congress—to battling to influence hundreds and thousands of decisions made at lower bureaucratic levels, decisions that draw on information available mainly at these levels.

Thus neglect of implementation does not arise simply from intellectual error, though there is a recurrent tendency of executives and their staffs to exaggerate the impact of their formal actions on real-life organizational processes. There is a deeper cause: the detailed work of implementation brings them onto ground where their bargaining advantages are few and the capacity of others to neutralize their actions is very great. Thus in terms of maximizing their own interests, executives and their staffs would devote great energy to implementation only if there were commensurate rewards. If in fact there were a political equivalent of the economic marketplace, and implementation of wisely designed organizational reforms led more or less clearly or visibly to greater market rewards, then it would be worth the effort. But this is seldom the case.

Moreover, the main rewards may lie outside the executive's time. A serious focus on implementation or organizational change means, in most instances, a commitment to evolution, to building up new systems and new competences slowly even if surely. Yet the tenure of the typical political executive will not permit such a priority.

Rewards do come, however, from expressing visible dissatisfaction with current organization and taking sweeping if superficial visible action with respect to it. Candidate Carter apparently saw substantial political gains from a high-visibility commitment with very generalized goals—making government more efficient and more compassionate. President Carter did not seem to have been damaged by the fact that his administration had not generated an exceptional amount of reorganization, much less by the fact that the jury is still out on whether his most visible new creations —the Departments of Energy and Education—are successful by any criterion other than symbolism and attractiveness to certain constituencies.

Such generalized stakes in the appearance of reorganization are hardly confined to Presidents. Three months after becoming Deputy Undersecretary of State for Administration, William B. Macomber launched his management "program for the seventies" with considerable public fanfare. Once his 13 task forces issued their reports, his staff gleaned from them 505 separate change proposals, and Macomber then issued a series of "Management Reform Bulletins" intended to publicize concrete progress in carrying them out. One intention may have been to maintain the momentum of reform, but the process degenerated into one where public relations took precedence over real achievement. Two hundred and fifty officials had served on the task forces, but in the implementation phase the same enormous range of problems were being tackled by only a handful of persons really committed to the program, most of them engaged part-time. They were almost inevitably driven to seek some degree of apparent compliance with as large a number of specific proposals as possible, and then to report this as success, which is exactly what they did. In the short run, this gave reformers their day in the sun, while also giving resisters and skeptics the assurance that little was really changing. Over time, of course, the credibility of the reform effort was substantially eroded, and the prospects for real system change were undercut. But the Deputy Undersecretary had already made his reputation as a reformer, and he was soon off to become Ambassador to Turkey.

Thus executives often get more rewards for appearing to reorganize than for actually doing so, or more from visible structural change than from reforms that actually achieve the specific reorganization goals. But even in the case of those who really want enduring change, there are barriers to giving implementation timely consideration.

Logically, attention to implementation should begin as soon as the general targets of likely reorganization are clear—people should be studying the real-life operating patterns of these agencies, discovering interests and sources of energy supporting change from within, assessing motivations of line officials and how they can work with or change these motivations, and building support for particular ideas before they are finally adopted. In pursuing this task, the general Carter administration priority to "bottom up" organizational studies has real merit. But moves that would prepare the way for prompt implementation—shifting personnel, canvassing office space, mobilizing congressional support—may be resisted for the simple reason that they tend to preempt the executive's decision, and to go beyond the mandate of the staffs or advisers working on reorganization. Lyndon Johnson explicitly told his reorganization task force that implementation was his job; they should concern themselves, in total confidentiality, with recommending what they thought was right. By contrast, one of the advantages of an ongoing reorganization staff like the President's Reorganization Project is that it can continue working on issues after the decision is made, and can see them through. But three years is probably not long enough, particularly if the President's commitment to organization change is perceived to be declining in the latter part of this period.

When a reorganization program is more lightly staffed, or when change proponents seize a sudden opportunity to win formal adoption of a proposal, there may be no advance effort aimed at implementation at all. As William Backus has written, the idea of establishing "country directors" as senior officials within the regional bureaus had long been considered at the State Department. But the actual order came suddenly, when Undersecretary U. Alexis Johnson and Deputy Undersecretary William Crockett seized the occasion of the President's issuance of NSAM 341 (establishing the Senior Interdepartmental Group) to get Secretary Rusk to approve that same day a State Department order (Foreign Affairs Manual Circular 385) creating the country director positions. This haste meant, apparently, that the reform was denied the impetus it might have gained from inclusion in the presidential order to which it was logically related. (Country directors were to be interagency leaders at their level just as the Undersecretary and Assistant Secretaries were to be under NSAM 341.)

More important, haste contributed to the fact that "the geographic assistant secretaries, whose bureaus were to be reorganized by the CD change, had little input into the decision process. . . . Thus those most affected by the change and most directly in a position to influence its success, with the possible exception of the CDs themselves, had little personal stake in the idea, and in some cases actually opposed it."[3] In fact, the reform had only limited success in practice. But this episode is one example of a recurrent pattern. Reformers maneuver to get the top executive to order a formal change, since it is the most important single step in advancing their cause. The executive does so as a one-shot action, either assuming that it will be self-executing or, more likely, because he is willing to do this small bit for those who propose it. But he does not follow through, does not reinforce implementation with his own behavior, does not work with those directly affected. This was the pattern with Rusk on the country directors, and with President Johnson, for the most part, on the SIG. Soon the reform loses credibility.

There seem to be only two types of organizational reforms where considerable resistance to implementation is not built in. One is where the action required follows straightforwardly from an authoritative decision— as in the Wriston case. Merger of the foreign and departmental services in State was highly controversial, but once the Secretary was ready to take it on, carrying it out required mainly central administrative persistence. And progress could be monitored by counting the number of department officials who became FSOs. The second is where the reorganization planners are themselves the implementers, as in the actions of successive administrations to reshape national security processes. In each case the national security assistant was responsible for recommending change to the President and carrying it through, whether it was Cutler under Eisenhower, Bundy under Kennedy, Kissinger under Nixon, or Brzezinski under Carter. And they were dealing with something they had considerable leverage over: how "presidential" national security issues would be staffed to provide a basis for presidential decisions. But while their formal (or, under Bundy, informal) systems operated more or less as designed, this did not make them identical to the Presidents' actual systems for making decisions. In fact, the greatest divergence came under the strongest national security adviser, Henry Kissinger, who in practice operated, with Nixon, a two-man, closed policy-making system on key issues, notwithstanding Nixon's declaration that his NSC system "insures that all agencies and departments receive a fair hearing before I make my decisions."

These two circumstances are not typical of reorganization. More often than not, its implementation requires discretionary decisions that cannot be controlled by executive decree (e.g., country directors behaving as leaders), decisions by those deep inside the agency whose processes are the target for change. And more often than not, the planners are not the implementers. In more normal circumstances, therefore, executives have to ask how constructive participation can be encouraged. How can senior career officials be brought to participate in shaping proposed changes so that they can share reform objectives and share responsibility and credit for their realization without the executive's very openness inviting excessive delay or sabotage? And students of the practice of reorganization must ask how executives and their staff analysts can develop a feel and a sympathy for the world of middle-level operations and shape reforms to relate to this world? How can executives be motivated to seek real change, over a sustained period? How can the rewards for superficial visible impact in one's own name be diminished, and the rewards for sticking with the job to accomplish something real be increased?

Such questions have no easy answers, if indeed they have answers at all. One necessary approach, also difficult to implement, must be to find ways to measure organizational change while it is taking place.

In a memo dated July 1971, an aide to Macomber expressed concern —well after his reform studies were completed and their implementation was under way—that "we have not yet established criteria for evaluation" of progress. This being the case, there was ultimately no way to distinguish paper compliance from real results. There was thus no way to reward systematically those bureaucrats who took the reform program seriously and worked for its fulfillment. Nor, absent such accepted measures, is the executive who opts for real organizational change likely to be recognized and rewarded either.

NOTES

1. Erwin Hargrove, "The Missing Link: The Study of the Implementation of Social Policy," Urban Institute, July 1975.
2. Stephen K. Bailey, "Managing the Federal Government," in Kermit Gordon, ed., *Agenda for the Nation* (Washington, D.C.: Brookings Institution, 1968), p. 319.
3. William Backus, *Foreign Policy and the Bureaucratic Process* (Princeton: Princeton University Press, 1974), p. 67.

# DATE DUE

DEC 15 1986

Snag 12/21/88